THE USBORNE
GEOGRAPHY
ENCYCLOPEDIA

Carol Varley and Lisa Miles

Designed by
**Fiona Brown, Nigel Reece
and Ruth Russell**

Illustrated by
**Guy Smith, Peter Dennis,
Chris Lyon, Peter Bull,
Kuo Kang Chen,
Wigwam Publishing Services
and Chris Shields**

Computer cartography by
EUROMAP Ltd

CHEROKEE SCHOOL
MEDIA CENTER

Additional illustration by
Mick Gillah and Derek Brazell

Geography consultants
Rex Walford, Bill Chambers
and Margaret Smeaton

Contents

About this book

Geography is the study of the Earth's surface and the people who live on it. This book introduces you to the world of geography. It is divided into thirteen sections of information.

Each section has a different coloured band along the tops of the pages. You can see what these sections are, and the colours used for them, in the Contents list opposite.

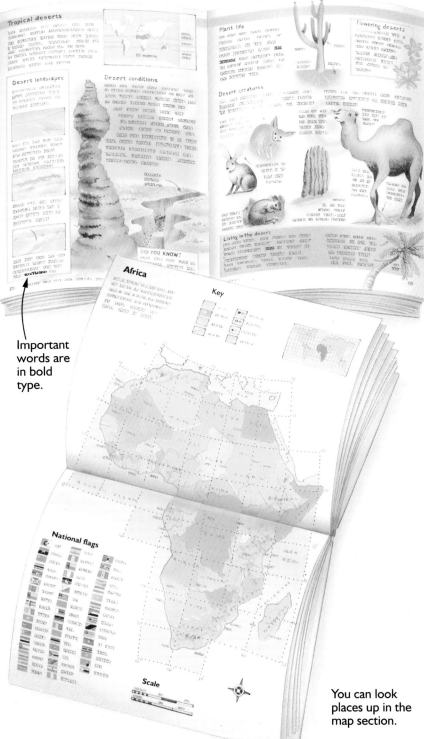

Important words are in bold type.

National flags

Africa

Key

Scale

You can look places up in the map section.

Important words

Some words are printed in bold type. These are important words which are explained at that point in the book.

Some words have an asterisk after them, like this – culture*. It means that this word is explained somewhere else in the book. The footnote at the bottom of the page tells you where.

Using the maps

There is also a map section, called Maps of the world. Each map in this section shows a different area of the world, its countries, major towns and cities, and its main features, such as mountains and rivers. These pages also show the national flags of each country.

The atlas maps have their own index, starting on page 118. When you come across place names in the book, you can look them up on the maps and find out exactly where they are in the world.

Looking up facts

There is a reference section on pages 110-128. You can use the reference section to look up lots of facts about the Earth and its countries.

It includes a glossary, where important words to do with geography are explained. There is also an index at the back of the book, so that you can find information easily.

*Culture, 55.

What is geography?

The word geography originally comes from the Greek word *geographia*, which means "writing about the Earth". It is a living subject about people and places and the relationship between people and the Earth.

The Earth and its inhabitants are always changing, so geography is also about how things change.

Geography may be split into two areas: physical geography, about the Earth and places; and human geography, about people and how they live. Together, they make a very broad subject. This book covers many aspects of geography, some of which are introduced on these two pages.

The planet Earth

Geography is about how the Earth moves in space, creating the days, nights and seasons. It is about how energy comes from the Sun so that animals and plants can live.

Weather patterns

Geographers study weather and climate change. They record and predict weather patterns and look at how the climate affects the way that people, animals and plants live.

Water and rocks

Water is essential to life on Earth. It forms part of the air around us and it covers part of the Earth's surface. Oceans shape the rocks on the coasts and rivers carve out features in the land.

Studying the oceans and the landscape helps people to understand how the Earth developed, how it may change in the future and how we can make better use of our surroundings.

People

Geographers study the people who live in the world, their lifestyles and their differences and similarities. Geography is about how the populations of different places change and how different societies work.

4

Settlements

Geography is about the places where people live and why they live there. It is about how communities grow and how villages, towns and cities have an impact on the environment around them.

Maps

Maps are an important part of geography. They show us where places are and what they are like. They help us to compare different places and understand our surroundings.

Using our surroundings

Geography shows how people use their surroundings for food, water and resources. It is about what jobs people do and how they change the world around them.

Communication

Geography is about how places around the world are linked together and how people communicate. It is about how transport systems and the landscape affect each other.

The environment

Geography is about how the environment is changed by everything that people do. It is about how fragile the Earth is and how we can conserve and protect our resources.

Why is geography important?

The population on Earth is growing and our way of life is changing faster than ever. Pollution levels are high and people are changing the Earth so much that its resources are in danger.

Geography is important because it helps us to understand why the landscape looks as it is does and why we live as we do. It explains the world we live in and shows us how we can use it effectively and protect it for the future.

The Earth, our planet

Our planet, Earth, is a large ball of rock and metal covered with water and soil. It belongs to a group of nine planets which travel around a star called the Sun. Together, the Sun and everything that travels around it is called the **Solar System**.

The planets of the Solar System travel along almost circular paths, called **orbits**. They also spin. The four planets nearest to the Sun are called the inner planets. Beyond them are the outer planets.

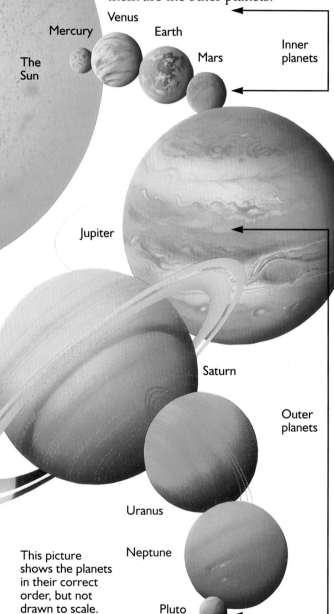

The Sun

Mercury

Venus

Earth

Mars

Inner planets

Jupiter

Saturn

Uranus

Neptune

Pluto

Outer planets

This picture shows the planets in their correct order, but not drawn to scale.

About the Earth

The Earth travels along its orbit at a speed of 107,200kmph (66,000mph). It also spins on its **axis**, an imaginary rod through the very north and south of the Earth, which leans at an angle of 23½°. The ends of the axis are called the **North Pole** and **South Pole**.

Around the Earth's middle, halfway between the Poles, is an imaginary line called the **Equator**. It divides the Earth into the **northern** and **southern hemispheres**.

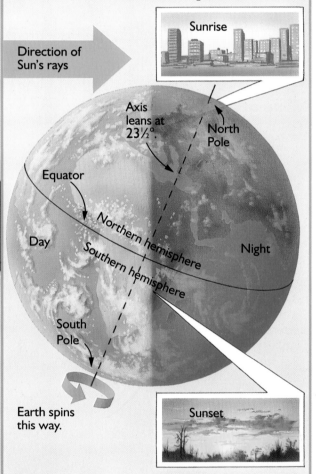

Direction of Sun's rays

Sunrise

Axis leans at 23½°.

North Pole

Equator

Northern hemisphere

Day

Southern hemisphere

Night

South Pole

Earth spins this way.

Sunset

It takes 24 hours (one day) for the Earth to spin once. As it spins, its surface passes through the Sun's rays (daylight) then turns towards the darkness of space (night).

Sunrise is when your part of the Earth turns towards the Sun. At sunset, the Sun seems to sink below the horizon as your part of the Earth turns away from its rays.

The year and seasons

It takes one year (365¼ days) for the Earth to orbit the Sun. Because the Earth is on a tilt, the northern hemisphere is tilted towards the Sun in June and the southern hemisphere is tilted towards the Sun in December. The hemisphere that is towards the Sun is in summer. The one tilted away is in winter.

Imaginary lines called the **Tropic of Cancer** and **Tropic of Capricorn**, north and south of the Equator, mark where the Sun's rays are most direct in June and December. In the picture below, the Tropics are shown by dotted lines. In spring and autumn (March and September), the Sun's rays are most direct at the Equator.

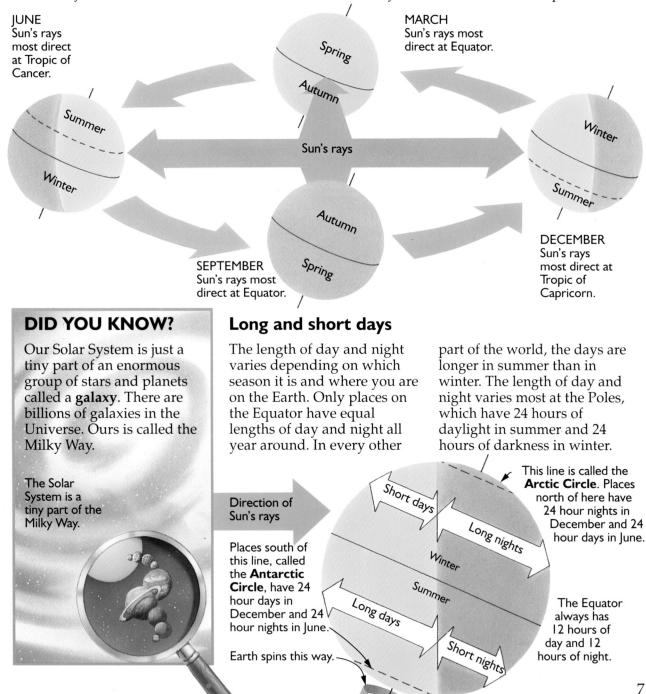

JUNE
Sun's rays most direct at Tropic of Cancer.

Summer

Winter

Spring

Autumn

Sun's rays

MARCH
Sun's rays most direct at Equator.

Winter

Summer

DECEMBER
Sun's rays most direct at Tropic of Capricorn.

Autumn

Spring

SEPTEMBER
Sun's rays most direct at Equator.

DID YOU KNOW?

Our Solar System is just a tiny part of an enormous group of stars and planets called a **galaxy**. There are billions of galaxies in the Universe. Ours is called the Milky Way.

The Solar System is a tiny part of the Milky Way.

Long and short days

The length of day and night varies depending on which season it is and where you are on the Earth. Only places on the Equator have equal lengths of day and night all year around. In every other part of the world, the days are longer in summer than in winter. The length of day and night varies most at the Poles, which have 24 hours of daylight in summer and 24 hours of darkness in winter.

Direction of Sun's rays

Places south of this line, called the **Antarctic Circle**, have 24 hour days in December and 24 hour nights in June.

Earth spins this way.

Short days

Long nights

Winter

Summer

Long days

Short nights

This line is called the **Arctic Circle**. Places north of here have 24 hour nights in December and 24 hour days in June.

The Equator always has 12 hours of day and 12 hours of night.

7

Mapping the Earth

To discover where places are on the Earth you need either a globe or a map. A globe is a model of the Earth, whereas maps show the Earth's surface as a flat sheet.

Lines around the globe

Lines drawn on a globe, called **lines of latitude** and **longitude**, help you to find where places are. You may see these lines on maps too.

Lines of longitude, or **meridians**, divide the Earth into segments like an orange. All lines of longitude meet at the Poles. Longitude is measured in degrees (°). The line through Greenwich, England is 0°. It is called the **Prime Meridian**. Lines to either side are measured in degrees east or west of the Prime Meridian.

Lines of latitude, or **parallels**, tell you how far north or south a place is. The Equator, around the Earth's middle, is 0° latitude. Lines of latitude north of the Equator are measured in degrees north (°N). Lines south of the Equator are measured in degrees south (°S). The Poles are 90° north and south of the Equator.

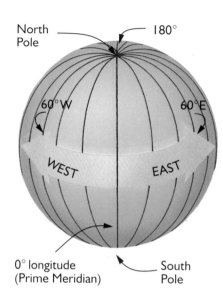

North Pole

180°

60°W

60°E

WEST

EAST

0° longitude (Prime Meridian)

South Pole

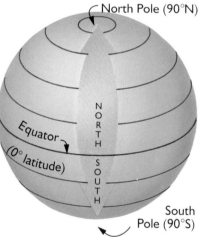

North Pole (90°N)

Equator (0° latitude)

NORTH

SOUTH

South Pole (90°S)

Where are you on the globe?

If you want to find a place on the globe, you will need to look up its latitude and longitude in the index of an atlas. For example, Madrid, in Spain, is 40°N, 3°W. This means it is 40° north of the Equator and 3° west of the Prime Meridian. Now follow the lines of latitude and longitude on a globe until they cross.

To be more precise, an atlas may give positions in degrees and minutes ('). A minute is one sixtieth of a degree. Madrid's exact position is 40°25'N, 3°43'W.

Flattening the Earth

Making a flat map of the Earth is like trying to flatten out an orange peel. For it to lie flat some parts would have to be stretched. Different areas of the Earth can be stretched to make it lie flat, so two world maps can look quite different from each other.

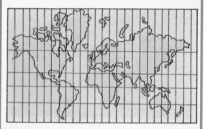

On this map, countries furthest from the Equator are stretched and this makes them look much bigger than they really are.

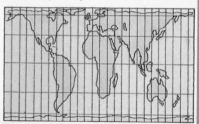

This map makes places near the Equator look much longer than they really are. Places near the Poles are squashed.

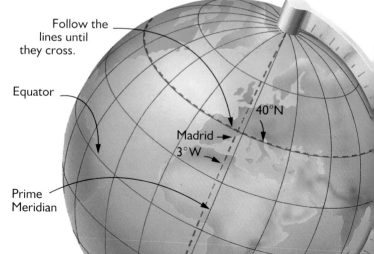

Follow the lines until they cross.

Equator

40°N

Madrid 3°W

Prime Meridian

The story of maps

People have been making maps since the early ages. The earliest maps anyone knows of were made by Babylonians and Egyptians over four thousand years ago. They were based on travellers' descriptions of places they had seen.

Early maps were carved into clay tablets.

Scholars in Ancient Greece worked out that the Earth is a sphere. The Greek geographer, Ptolemy, worked out distances between places by studying the positions of the stars and collecting information from travellers.

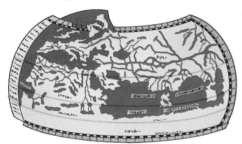

When Ptolemy created this map of the world, he thought Europe, Asia and Africa were the only continents.

Over the past thousand years, many explorers have set out by land and sea to discover the world. In 1787 the theodolite was invented. This is a telescope with a device for measuring angles. It makes map-making easier.

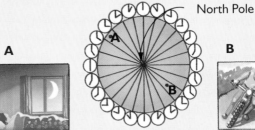

16th century theodolite

Satellite maps such as this can show every part of the Earth's surface.

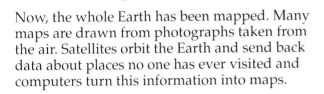

Now, the whole Earth has been mapped. Many maps are drawn from photographs taken from the air. Satellites orbit the Earth and send back data about places no one has ever visited and computers turn this information into maps.

24 hour globe

The Earth has been divided into 24 time zones. Without them no one would know what time it is anywhere else in the world. The zones roughly follow lines of longitude.

In each time zone, people set their clocks and watches to their own standard time. The picture below shows how standard time varies around the world. For example, when the standard time at A is 3.00 in the morning, the standard time at B is 3.00 in the afternoon.

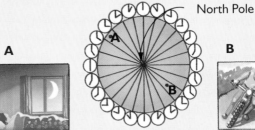

North Pole

A

B

If you travel east or west into a different time zone you have to alter the time on your watch to the standard time in the new zone. If you cross a time zone travelling east, put your watch forward. If you cross a time zone travelling west, put your watch back.

Move watch back travelling west.

Move watch forward travelling east.

The 180° line of longitude is called the **International Date Line**. Places just west of this line are 24 hours ahead of places just to the east. If you cross it, the time stays the same but you gain or lose a whole day.

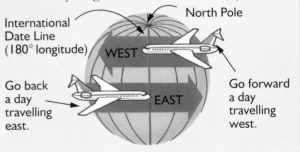

International Date Line (180° longitude)

North Pole

WEST

Go back a day travelling east.

EAST

Go forward a day travelling west.

Looking at maps

To show even a tiny part of the Earth's surface on a map, it usually has to be drawn much smaller than it really is. Drawing something smaller or larger than it is and keeping it all in proportion is called **drawing to scale**. The smaller something is drawn, the smaller the scale.

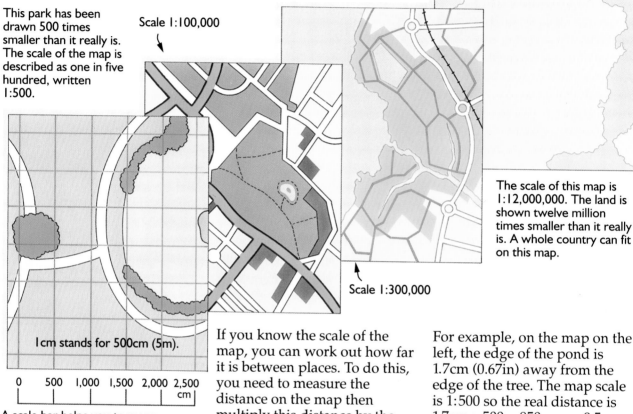

This park has been drawn 500 times smaller than it really is. The scale of the map is described as one in five hundred, written 1:500.

Scale 1:100,000

Scale 1:300,000

1cm stands for 500cm (5m).

| 0 | 500 | 1,000 | 1,500 | 2,000 | 2,500 |

cm

A scale bar helps you to measure distances on a map.

The scale of this map is 1:12,000,000. The land is shown twelve million times smaller than it really is. A whole country can fit on this map.

If you know the scale of the map, you can work out how far it is between places. To do this, you need to measure the distance on the map then multiply this distance by the scale of the map.

For example, on the map on the left, the edge of the pond is 1.7cm (0.67in) away from the edge of the tree. The map scale is 1:500 so the real distance is 1.7cm x 500 = 850cm, or 8.5m (9.3yd).

Sign language

A small scale map is like a view from high above the Earth. If everything was drawn as it really looked, most things in the landscape would be far too small for you to see.

So that you can see features more clearly, map-makers (cartographers) show them as symbols. These are called conventional signs. A **key** to the map tells you what the symbols mean.

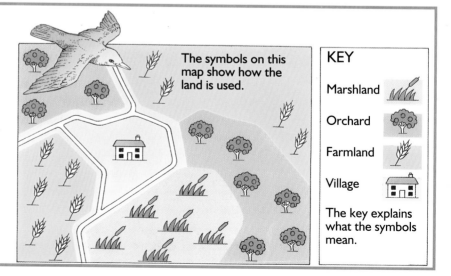

The symbols on this map show how the land is used.

KEY

Marshland

Orchard

Farmland

Village

The key explains what the symbols mean.

How hilly is it?

Surveyors, who study the shape of the land, have equipment to measure how high it is. They work out how far it rises above sea-level. The easiest way to show how the land rises is with a side-on drawing called a **cross-section**.

When cartographers draw maps, they have to show the shape of the land from above. One way to do this is with lines called **contours**. Contours join up all the places on the map that are the same height above sea-level. Small numbers on or next to the contours tell you what height they stand for.

On some maps, spaces between contours are coloured in different shades. This is called **layer tinting**. A key tells you what heights the colours stand for. Layer tinting makes it easier to see where the land is highest.

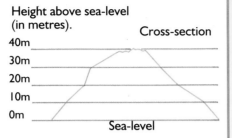

Height above sea-level (in metres).

Cross-section

40m
30m
20m
10m
0m

Sea-level

Contours join up places of same height.

30m 40m
20m
10m
0m

Key shows what height the colours stand for.

40m
30m
20m
10m
0m

Types of slope

Here are some slopes you might find in a landscape and the patterns they make when they are shown as contours on a map.

Steady slope

Steady slopes have evenly spaced contours.

Concave slope

A **concave** slope is gentle at the bottom but becomes much steeper higher up. The contours are closer together where the land is steeper.

Convex slope

A **convex** slope rises very steeply but becomes more gentle higher up.

How long will it take to walk?

If you are planning a walk, you will probably need a map to help you decide the route. Using the scale and contours, you can work out how long the walk will take.

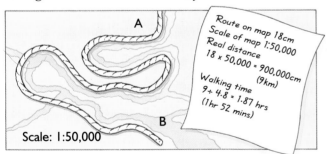

A

B

Scale: 1:50,000

Route on map 18cm
Scale of map 1:50,000
Real distance
18 x 50,000 = 900,000cm
(9km)

Walking time
9 ÷ 4.8 = 1.87 hrs
(1hr 52 mins)

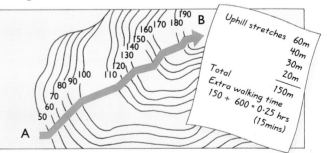

190 B
160 170 180
150
140
130
120
100 110
80 90
70
60
50
A

Uphill stretches 60m
40m
30m
20m
———
Total 150m
Extra walking time
150 ÷ 600 = 0.25 hrs
(15mins)

If the walk is across flat ground, measure the route on the map. To do this you could lay a piece of string along the route. Now use the method described on the opposite page to calculate the real distance. Most people walk at a speed of 4.8km (3 miles) per hour, so divide the walking distance by this figure to work out how long the walk will take.

A hilly walk will take longer than a flat one. To calculate how much longer, you need to work out how far you will climb. Follow your route on a map. Each time you cross a contour line going uphill, note how much the land rises. Add up the figures and, for every 600m (2,000ft) you climb, add one hour to your journey. Downhill stretches count as flat.

11

Using maps

When reading a map, you can find out which direction is which by using a compass. The compass needle is turned by the Earth's magnetic force* so that it always points towards north. The eight main points of a compass, called the **cardinal points**, are marked around the edge of the compass dial. The dial is also split up into 360 degrees (°). If you turn the dial so that the N for north lines up with the compass needle, you can work out the direction of things around you.

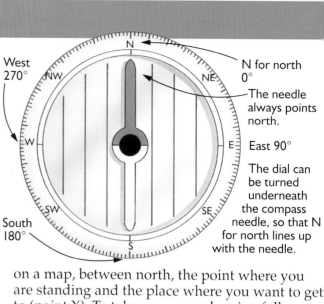

West 270°

South 180°

N for north 0°

The needle always points north.

East 90°

The dial can be turned underneath the compass needle, so that N for north lines up with the needle.

Finding your way

To find your way to a place (point X), which you cannot yet see in the distance, you can work out in which direction to go by taking a **compass bearing**. This is the angle, measured in degrees on a map, between north, the point where you are standing and the place where you want to get to (point X). To take a compass bearing follow the instructions below.

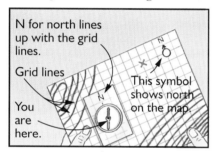

N for north lines up with the grid lines.

Grid lines

This symbol shows north on the map.

You are here.

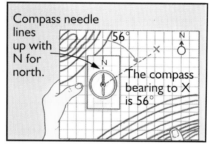

Compass needle lines up with N for north.

56°

The compass bearing to X is 56°.

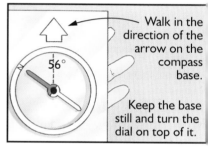

Walk in the direction of the arrow on the compass base.

56°

Keep the base still and turn the dial on top of it.

1. Look at the map to find out where you are, and place the compass on that point. Turn the dial of the compass around so that N for north lines up with the vertical grid lines. These run from north to south on the map.

2. Turn your body and the map around until the needle lines up with N for north. Imagine a line between X and the middle of the compass. The place at which this line crosses the dial shows the direction or compass bearing to follow.

3. Turn the dial so that the compass bearing lines up with the arrow on the compass base. Turn around until the needle lines up with N for north. Walk forward, making sure that the needle stays level with N for north.

Grid references

The grid squares on a map are given numbers or letters. You can find places by knowing the number or the letter of the square where they are found. This is called the **grid reference**. On the map on the right, Newtown is in the square next to the vertical line 02 and the horizontal line 13. Giving the vertical line first, Newtown's grid reference is 0213.

For accuracy, the space between the grid lines may be split into ten. Newtown station is at point 026132, because it is 6 spaces along and 2 spaces up in square 0213.

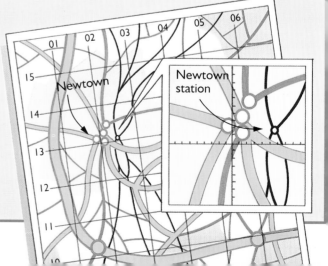

Newtown

Newtown station

12   *Earth's magnetic force, 15.*

How to make a map

Anyone can make a map. You could start by making a map of a room or a garden. Here are some simple steps to follow.

First, you need to measure the area by pacing along each side. Choose a scale* for the map, for example 1cm (½in) for each pace. Draw the edges of the area on paper. Use a pencil in case you need to erase any mistakes.

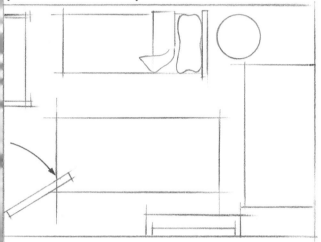

Now work out the sizes and positions of the main features and draw them in. For example, if you are mapping a room, draw the doors, windows and large pieces of furniture. Draw them as if you are looking down from above.

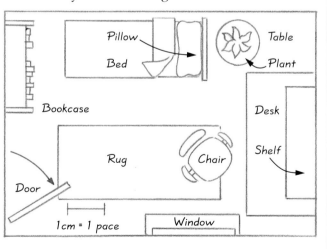

Next, fill in the smaller features between the main ones. For example, add in things such as a bedside table or a plant.

Last, label everything on the map. Also write the scale that you have used on the map.

*Scale, 10.

Types of maps

Different types of maps have different uses. Tourist maps, for instance, have symbols to show places of interest in a certain area.

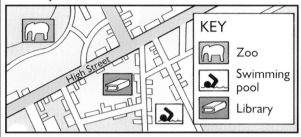

Road maps show large areas so that people can plan long journeys. The different types of roads are shown in different colours.

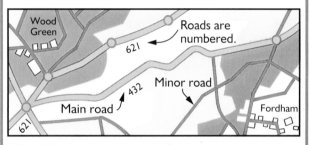

Distribution maps use colours or symbols to show facts about a particular area, for example where different languages are spoken.

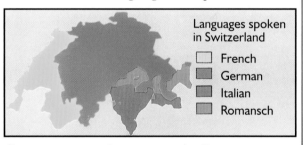

Some maps, such as maps of railway systems, show each part of the route as a straight line. The detail is left out, which makes them easy to read.

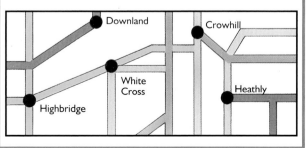

What the Earth is made of

The Earth began 4,500 million years ago as a ball of gases. Gradually, heavy metals sank to the centre and solidified. Lighter rocks and minerals* floated to the surface, cooled and hardened.

Heavy metals such as iron and nickel sank to the Earth's centre.

Earth 4,500 million years ago. ↓

The Earth began as gases.

The gases became solid minerals.

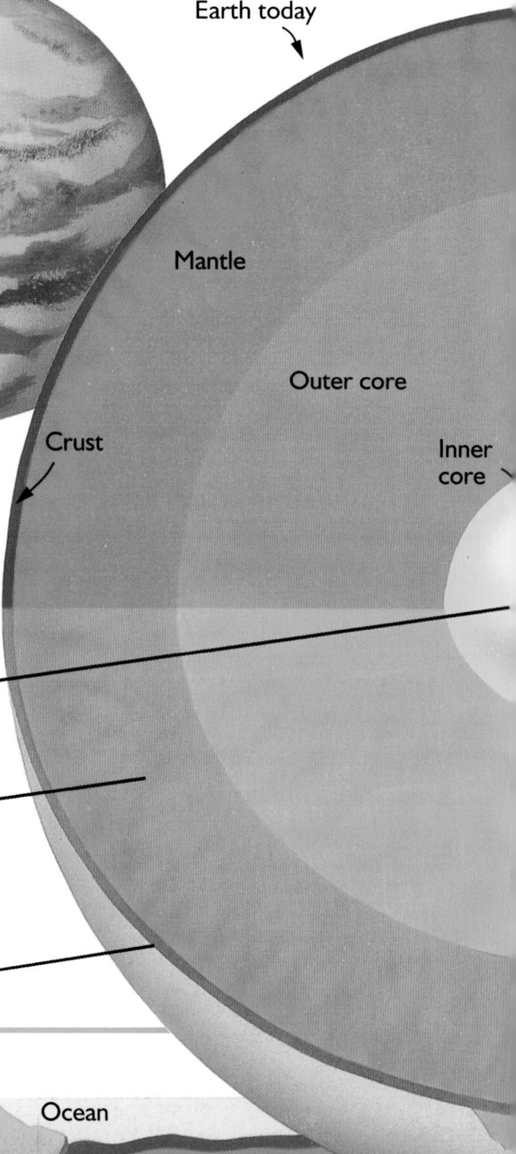

Earth today ↘

Mantle

Outer core

Crust

Inner core

Slicing through the Earth

If you sliced through the Earth you would see three layers: the **core** in the middle, the **mantle** surrounding the core, and a hard outer shell called the **crust**.

The core has two layers. The inner core is made of solid iron and nickel and the outer core of liquid (molten) iron and nickel.

The mantle is made of rock. The upper part is semi-molten rock, called **magma**.

The crust is the thinnest of the three layers. If you imagine the Earth as a tennis ball, the crust would be thinner than a postage stamp attached to its surface.

A close-up of the crust

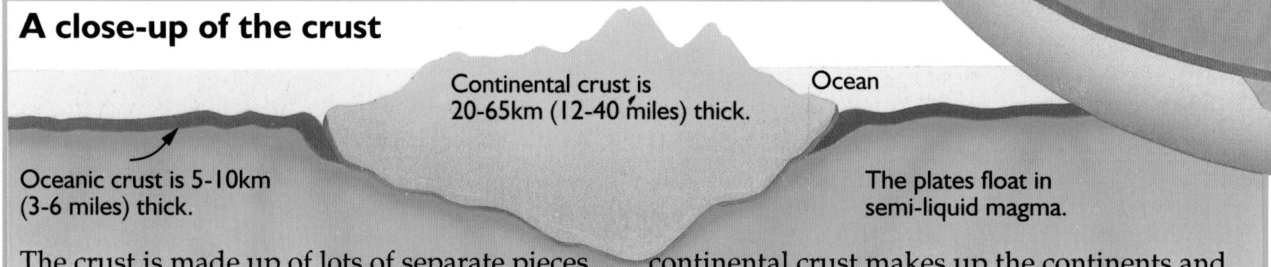

Continental crust is 20-65km (12-40 miles) thick.

Ocean

Oceanic crust is 5-10km (3-6 miles) thick.

The plates float in semi-liquid magma.

The crust is made up of lots of separate pieces, called **plates**, which fit together rather like an enormous jigsaw puzzle. The plates float in the semi-molten upper mantle.

There are two different types of crust; thick continental crust makes up the continents and much thinner oceanic crust makes up the ocean floors. Continental crust is made of granite, which is a light rock. Oceanic crust is made of dense basalt rock.

Investigating the Earth

It is not easy finding out about the inside of the Earth. Geologists, who study rocks, have tried drilling holes in the crust to collect rock samples but there is no drill big enough to go more than a short distance below the Earth's surface. To find out what is deeper down, geologists study records of earthquakes*, called seismographs. During an earthquake, vibrations called seismic waves travel through the Earth, and as they pass through different types of rock, the waves change speed and direction (see picture below). By studying seismographs, it is possible to work out what the rocks are like at different depths.

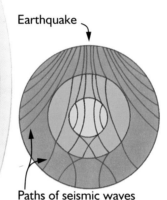

Earthquake

The atmosphere

Paths of seismic waves

The Earth's blanket

As the Earth formed, gases escaped and settled in layers around its surface. These gases are the **atmosphere**.

Without the atmosphere, nothing could live on Earth. It contains a thin layer of gas, called the **ozone layer**, which filters out harmful rays from the Sun. It also contains the gases we need to breathe. It has other uses too. For example, radio waves can be bounced off layers of dust in the atmosphere to different parts of the world.

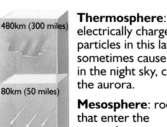

480km (300 miles)

80km (50 miles)

50km (30 miles)

11km (7 miles)

Thermosphere: electrically charged particles in this layer sometimes cause lights in the night sky, called the aurora.

Mesosphere: rocks that enter the atmosphere (meteorites), burn up in this layer.

Stratosphere: jets fly in this layer because it is very still.

Troposphere: weather happens in this layer.

Magnetic Earth

The Earth is magnetic. It is as though a giant magnetic rod runs through its core. The ends of the magnet are called the **magnetic poles**.

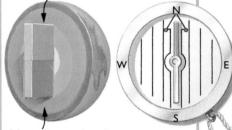

Magnetic north pole

Magnetic south pole

You can see the Earth's magnetic force at work if you use a compass. The compass needle, which is also magnetic, is pulled by the Earth's magnetic force so it always points to the Earth's magnetic north pole.

The Earth's pull

Gravity is a force that pulls objects towards each other. It holds you and everything around you on the Earth's surface.

Pull of Earth's gravity

Gravity is strongest at the centre of the Earth. The further something is from the Earth's centre, the weaker the pull. Gravity is weaker at the top of a mountain than the bottom, for example.

*Earthquakes, 18.

The restless Earth

The plates of the Earth's crust* are always moving – gradually pushing together, pulling apart or sliding past each other. These plate movements are caused by currents of magma* (molten rock) beneath the crust. Heat from the Earth's core* warms the magma and makes it rise. It pushes against the plates and drags them along.

Where two plates are pulled apart, hot magma oozes up to fill the gap. As it cools, it sets to form new rock. These areas, where new rock is being made, are called **constructive plate boundaries**. The new rock may form a **ridge** along the plate boundary. For example, the Mid-Atlantic Ridge, which runs beneath the Atlantic Ocean* (see map below) has formed in this way.

As plates move apart in one area, they push together in another. One plate slides over the other and the lower one disappears into the magma, where it eventually melts. The groove where the plates meet is called a **trench**. These boundaries are called **destructive plate boundaries**.

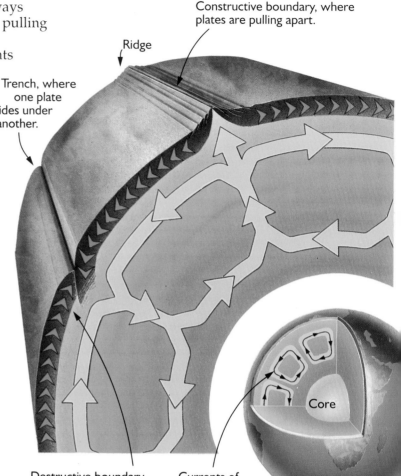

Constructive boundary, where plates are pulling apart.

Ridge

Trench, where one plate slides under another.

Destructive boundary, where plates are pushing together.

Currents of hot magma

Core

Where are the boundaries?

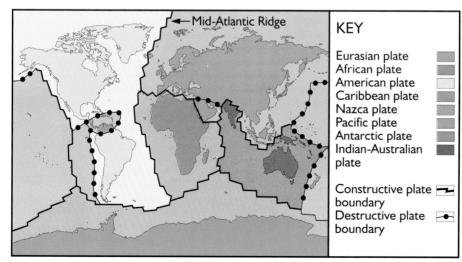

←Mid-Atlantic Ridge

KEY

Eurasian plate
African plate
American plate
Caribbean plate
Nazca plate
Pacific plate
Antarctic plate
Indian-Australian plate

Constructive plate boundary
Destructive plate boundary

The map on the left shows the positions of the world's constructive and destructive plate boundaries. The movement of the plates in these areas has caused many of the world's mountain ranges to form there. The Earth's crust is weaker along the plate boundaries, so most of the world's volcanoes and earthquakes occur in these areas too. You can find out about these over the page.

*Core, crust, magma, 14; oceans, 24.

Drifting continents

The plates move very slowly – only about a hand's width a year. Over millions of years, however, this is enough to make continents drift huge distances, as these maps show.

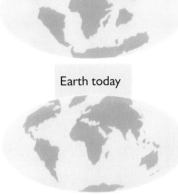

Earth 200 million years ago

Earth 135 million years ago

Earth 65 million years ago

Earth today

The continents are still drifting. Every year the Pacific Ocean is 9cm (3.5in) wider. In 50 million years, the shapes and positions of the continents will be quite different from today.

Fold mountains

Many of the world's highest mountain ranges are **fold mountains**. They began to form millions of years ago when plates pushed together under the oceans.

As one plate slid beneath the other, particles of rock (sediment) on the seabed piled up. Heat and pressure gradually turned the sediment to solid sedimentary rock*.

The Himalayas, Andes and Alps are all chains of fold mountains. Some mountains, such as Mount Everest in the Himalayas, are still growing in this way.

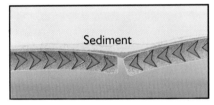

Sediment

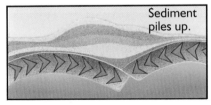

Sediment piles up.

The Himalayas

Crust under pressure

If pressure builds up under the Earth's surface, brittle rocks in the crust may crack. Cracks in rocks are called **faults**.

If two faults occur close together, the chunk of crust between them may be pushed up or slip down below the surrounding rock. Chunks that are pushed up are called **block mountains** or **horsts**. A low area between two horsts is called a **rift valley**.

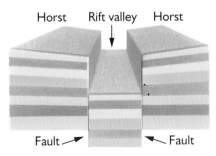

Horst   Rift valley   Horst

Fault   Fault

The most famous rift valley is the Rift Valley in East Africa. The Rhine Valley in Germany and Death Valley in the USA are also rift valleys.

In some areas, currents of magma under the crust flow together from opposite directions. The pressure may squeeze the crust and make it buckle and form **folds** such as those shown here.

Simple folds

Recumbent fold, where rocks form a pleat.

Magma flowing opposite ways.

Overfold, where rocks lean over gently.

*Sedimentary rocks, 20.

17

Earthquakes and volcanoes

Activity along the Earth's plate boundaries* is usually very slow but sometimes pressure builds up underground and causes dramatic earthquakes and volcanic eruptions.

Earthquakes occur where two plates slide past each other and their jagged edges jam. Strain builds up until one plate finally gives way and there is a sudden movement, which makes the earth shudder or quake.

The actual point where the rocks move is usually about 5-15km (3-10 miles) underground. It is called the **focus** of the earthquake. The point on the Earth's surface directly above the focus is called the **epicentre**.

The vibrations of an earthquake are called **seismic waves**. They are strongest at the focus and become weaker as they spread out.

Epicentre

Seismic waves

Focus, where jammed plates lunge past each other.

Seismic waves from even a small earthquake can be detected on the other side of the world.

Making records

People who study earthquakes are called seismologists. The instrument they use to measure seismic waves is called a seismometer. It has a revolving drum and a suspended pen fixed to a weight. During an earthquake the drum shakes and the pen draws a chart called a seismograph.

Drum shakes.

Weight and pen stay still.

Pen draws seismograph.

Taking precautions

Seismologists try to predict where and when earthquakes may happen so that people can be prepared. An earthquake can sometimes be prevented by injecting water into the rocks to release the jammed plates. Also, a small explosion can make the plates move before too much stress builds up.

Measuring earthquakes

There are two scales for measuring earthquakes. The **Richter Scale** measures the power of the seismic waves. The **Mercalli Scale**, described on the right, measures the effects of the earthquake on people and buildings.

A weak earthquake may be more serious than a very powerful one if it happens in a city where there are a lot of buildings and people.

Mercalli Scale

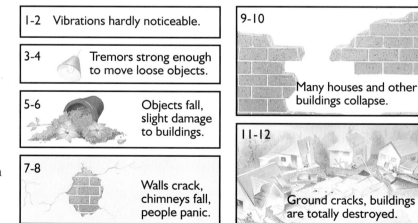

1-2 Vibrations hardly noticeable.

3-4 Tremors strong enough to move loose objects.

5-6 Objects fall, slight damage to buildings.

7-8 Walls crack, chimneys fall, people panic.

9-10 Many houses and other buildings collapse.

11-12 Ground cracks, buildings are totally destroyed.

What is a volcano?

There are about 600 volcanoes in the world. Most are found at weak points along plate boundaries, where red-hot magma* rises up from within the Earth and reaches the surface.

A typical volcano is a mound with a pipe, or **vent**, down the middle and a **magma chamber** below. Channels called **sills** and **dykes** may also lead from the magma chamber. When pressure builds up in the magma chamber, a mixture of magma and solid rock, called **lava**, pushes up the vent and the volcano erupts. If the lava is very thick it may set inside the vent and form a plug. Great pressure builds up and finally explodes the plug, hurling chunks of rock called volcanic bombs high into the air. If lava is thin, it erupts much more gently.

Each time a volcano erupts, the lava sets as a solid layer. As the layers build up, the volcano grows. Thick lava flows only a short way before setting so it forms steep-sided **cone volcanoes**. Thin lava flows further before it sets, so it forms volcanoes with gently sloping sides. These are called **shield volcanoes**.

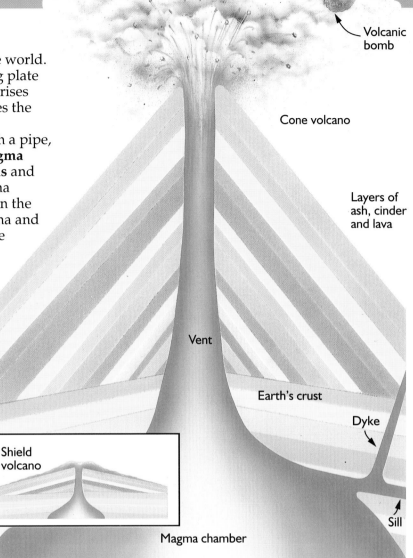

Volcanic bomb

Cone volcano

Layers of ash, cinder and lava

Vent

Earth's crust

Dyke

Sill

Shield volcano

Magma chamber

Hot water

If underground water is close to magma, it becomes extremely hot and may rise up and erupt. It may spurt out of the ground as a jet of super-heated water called a **geyser** or as a jet of steam called a **fumarole**. Mud pools form if steam bubbles through volcanic ash.

Mud pool

Alive, asleep or dead?

Volcanoes that erupt regularly are called active volcanoes. Volcanoes that will never erupt again are extinct. It may be difficult to tell if a volcano is extinct or whether it is sleeping (dormant). In 1973, for example, the volcano on the island of Heimaey, near Iceland, erupted and destroyed 300 buildings. Everyone thought it was extinct because it had not erupted for over 5,000 years .

Undersea volcanoes

Many volcanoes are under the sea. Some grow so big that they emerge above sea-level as new islands. Iceland is a volcanic island. It is still growing with each eruption.

*Magma, 14.

Rocks and minerals

The Earth's crust* is made up of rocks. Many are millions of years old but new rocks are being created all the time. There are three categories of rocks: sedimentary rocks, metamorphic rocks and igneous rocks.

Landscape is weathered (worn away), into small fragments.

Extinct volcano

Sediment is carried down to the seabed and layers of sedimentary rock build up.

Layers of volcanic ash

Extrusive igneous rock

Metamorphic rocks

Sedimentary rocks

Intrusive igneous rock

Chalk is made from shells of tiny sea creatures.

Shale is solidified mud or clay.

Sandstone is made of fragments of rock.

Sedimentary rocks form from fragments of rock, plants and animals that are washed or blown from the landscape. The fragments (sediment) settle, usually on the seabed. As layers build up, deeper sediment is squeezed tightly and eventually turns into solid rock.

Marble is a hard metamorphic rock formed from chalk.

Slate is a layered metamorphic rock formed from shale.

Metamorphic rocks are rocks that have been changed by heat or pressure. They may have been baked by heat from a nearby magma chamber* or forced together by movement within the crust. Some rocks become very hard, others are rearranged into fine layers.

Granite is the most common intrusive igneous rock.

Basalt is an extrusive igneous rock.

Igneous rocks form when magma from inside the Earth cools and sets. If it sets underground, the rocks are called **intrusive igneous rocks**. If magma spills out through volcanoes* or gaps in the crust and sets on the surface, it forms **extrusive igneous rock**.

Recycled rocks

As ancient rocks in the landscape wear down, their sediment helps to make new rocks, so rocks are always being renewed. The new sedimentary rocks may be buried for many millions of years. During this time they may be baked or squashed to form metamorphic rocks, or melted then cooled to form igneous rocks. Sooner or later, movements in the crust will heave the rocks back up to the surface and the process will begin again.

*Crust, 14; magma chamber, volcanoes, 19.

Mineral ingredients

Rocks are made of basic ingredients called **minerals**. Some rocks are made of just one mineral but most rocks are made of two or more minerals. Granite, for example, is made of quartz, mica and felspar. If you look at a piece of rock under a magnifying glass, you may be able to see the different minerals that it is made of.

Lump of granite

Magnified granite

White areas are quartz.

Black areas are mica.

Pinkish areas are felspar.

Buried treasure

Valuable, pure minerals may be found within rocks. Many form as shapeless lumps, some collect within cracks and form veins. If there is plenty of space, some minerals form beautiful, angular crystals. Different minerals form different shaped crystals.

Quartz crystal

Vein of turquoise

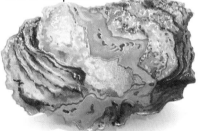

Lump of hematite (iron ore)

What are fossils?

Fossils are found inside certain rocks. They are the preserved shapes of things that were once alive.

Dead sea-creature

Seabed

Fossils form when sediment settles on top of dead plants and animals and turns to rock around them.

Sediment builds up.

The plant or animal may be preserved whole within the rock but usually it decays and the space it leaves is filled with minerals.

Fossils tell us what lived on Earth millions of years ago.

Minerals around you

Minerals are mined and used to make many everyday things. Here are some examples.

Match heads are made of sulphur, which burns easily.

Many fireworks contain barium, which burns with a green flame.

Pencil leads contain graphite, which marks things easily.

Sandpaper is coated with grains of a hard mineral called corundum.

Talcum powder is a ground up, absorbent mineral called talc.

Table salt is a mineral called halite.

Weathering

The rocks in the landscape are constantly being worn down by rain and temperature changes. This is called **weathering**.

There are two types of weathering. One type, called **mechanical weathering**, happens when water in rock crevices freezes. When water freezes, it expands (swells) and gradually breaks the rock apart.

Mechanical weathering happens fastest in areas where the temperature often rises and falls above and below freezing point, such as the Poles, mountain tops and deserts*.

Water in cracks expands when it freezes, breaking off chunks of rock.

Sharp pieces of weathered rocks, called **scree**, may collect at the base of a slope.

The other type of weathering is called **chemical weathering**. This is caused by rain-water or water in the soil, which are weak acids. The rock surface dissolves as the water trickles over it.

Some types of rock dissolve much more easily than others. It depends which minerals* the rock is made of. Also, rocks with lots of cracks weather fast because there are plenty of places for water and frost to work their way in.

Water trickles between cracks and dissolves the rock.

Products of weathering

When rocks are weathered, they break into smaller and smaller pieces.

Rock breaks into large blocks called **clasts**.

Or layers of rock peel away in thin sheets. This is called **exfoliation**.

The surface then wears into individual sand-sized grains.

Sand gradually wears down into tiny particles.

These particles become smaller and smaller and smaller...

Weathering and soil

Soil contains particles from the weathered rock below, such as clay, sand and minerals such as calcium and magnesium. These are mixed with decaying plant and animal matter, air and water. If you dug down through the ground to the rock you would see that soil has several layers, or **horizons**.

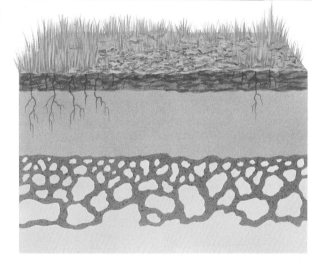

Surface layer of plant and animal remains, called **leaf litter**.

Top soil where leaf litter has decayed and mixed with minerals from the rock.

Sub-soil, mainly made up of weathered rock and a small amount of plant matter.

Unweathered rock, called **parent material**.

Landscape detective

Different types of rock weather at different rates. It is sometimes possible to identify rocks in the landscape by studying the way they have worn down and the features that are left.

Igneous rocks* such as granite are very tough and weather slowly. Weaker surrounding rocks wear down more quickly. At the sites of ancient volcanoes*, solidified magma chambers* called **batholiths** may be exposed and stand as huge mounds. Sills* and dykes* may stick out as ridges, and piles of granite boulders, called **tors**, may be left standing on hilltops.

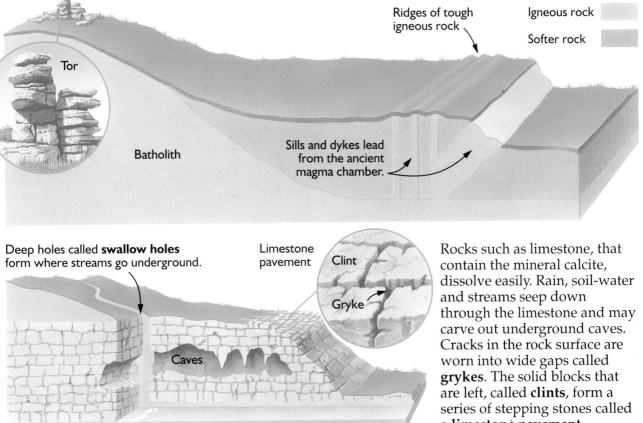

Tor

Batholith

Ridges of tough igneous rock

Sills and dykes lead from the ancient magma chamber.

Igneous rock

Softer rock

Deep holes called **swallow holes** form where streams go underground.

Limestone pavement

Clint

Gryke

Caves

Rocks such as limestone, that contain the mineral calcite, dissolve easily. Rain, soil-water and streams seep down through the limestone and may carve out underground caves. Cracks in the rock surface are worn into wide gaps called **grykes**. The solid blocks that are left, called **clints**, form a series of stepping stones called a **limestone pavement**.

Weathering around town

Weathering does not only affect the landscape – stone buildings and statues wear away too.

One way to study the effects of weathering is to compare tombstones of different ages. The dates on the stones make it easy to work out how long the rain and frost have been wearing them away.

This statue of Queen Victoria in London, England, was so badly weathered that the nose crumbled away and had to be replaced.

Weathered tombstones

*Dykes, 19; igneous rock, 20; magma chamber, sills, volcanoes, 19.

Oceans

Water covers almost three quarters of the Earth's surface. Over 97% of all this water is stored in the Earth's four huge oceans: the Pacific, Atlantic, Indian and Arctic Oceans.

Exploring the seabed

The shallowest parts of the oceans are the **continental shelves**, where land slopes gently down into the water. There is then a steep slope, called the **continental slope**, leading to the ocean floor, or **abyssal plain**.

Some of the Earth's most spectacular land formations are found on the ocean floor. Deep trenches* and huge ridges* run across it. Some stretch for over 60,000km (37,300 miles).

How the oceans formed

The Earth has not always had oceans. Millions of years ago it was just a ball of hot rock. Its surface was covered with erupting volcanoes*, which released huge amounts of gas, including a gas made up of water particles, called **water vapour**.

Eventually the Earth cooled, causing the water vapour to turn back into liquid water and fall from the skies as torrential rain. The rain lasted for thousands and thousands of years and gradually filled all the hollows around the Earth's surface, forming the oceans and seas.

Deep valleys called **submarine canyons** cut through the continental slope.

Volcano

Continental shelf. The ocean here is no more than 180m (590ft) deep.

The abyssal plain is about 5,000m (16,400ft) deep.

Seamounts

A continental shelf may stretch more than 300km (185 miles) away from the land.

Continental slope

Guyots

Deep troughs run along the middle of oceanic ridges.

Mid-oceanic ridges are caused by the plates of the Earth's crust pulling apart.

Trenches form where plates of the Earth's crust are pushing together.

The Earth's crust is thinner and more fragile underneath the oceans, so many volcanoes form at weak points. There are also huge mountains called **seamounts**, which may be up to 1,000m (3,280ft) high. Some, called **guyots**, have flattened peaks because they have been gradually eroded (worn away) by the movement of the water above.

Earth's crust, 14; ridges, trenches, 16; volcanoes, 19.

Restless water

The water in the oceans is constantly moving in currents, waves and tides. **Currents** are wide bands of water that flow around the oceans in huge circles. They are caused by global winds*, which gradually drag the water along with them. The Earth's spin makes currents swing to the side.

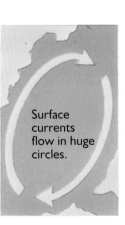

Surface currents flow in huge circles.

Waves are caused by the wind blowing across the surface of the water. The water does not move along with the waves, though – it is blown up into a crest, then falls down and back again in a circle. This is why an object floating in the waves bobs up and down but does not move along.

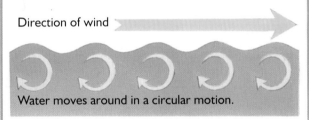

Direction of wind

Water moves around in a circular motion.

Tides are the rise and fall of the sea-level. High tide is when the water comes way up the shore. Low tide is when the sea is a long way out. Tides are caused by the Sun and Moon's gravity* pulling on the Earth's oceans.

When the Sun and Moon are in line with each other, their gravity pulls together on the oceans so there is a big difference between high and low tide. This is called a **spring tide**. Spring tides occur every 14 days.

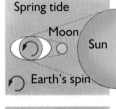

Spring tide

Moon

Sun

Earth's spin

When the Sun and Moon are at right angles to each other, the pull of one almost cancels out the pull of the other, so there is less difference between high and low tide. This is called a **neap tide**. Neap tides occur halfway between spring tides.

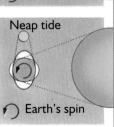

Neap tide

Earth's spin

Global winds, 34; gravity, 15.

Ocean layers

The temperature of the oceans changes with depth. The surface is the warmest layer because it is heated by the Sun's rays. This is called the **sunlight zone**.

As the water moves around in waves and surface currents, warm water mixes with cooler water below so the warmth spreads downwards into the next layer, called the **twilight zone**. Below this is a cold, dark layer, where the water is very still.

In the deepest parts of the ocean – the trenches – the water is icy-cold and there is no light at all.

Surface

Sunlight zone 200m (656ft)

Twilight zone 1,000m (3,280ft)

Dark zone 6,000m (19,685ft)

Deepest level 11,000m (36,090ft)

DID YOU KNOW?

The deepest part of the ocean is the Mariana Trench in the Pacific Ocean. It is 11,034m (36,200ft) deep. Mount Everest could fit inside without its peak poking out.

Giant waves

Earthquakes, landslides and volcanic eruptions under the ocean can create giant waves, called **tsunami**. These waves (sometimes wrongly called tidal waves) can be over 60m (200ft) high and travel at speeds of up to 800kmph (500mph).

Tsunami are most common in Japan where they come in from the Pacific Ocean.

Water on the land

Water can be a liquid, a solid (ice) or a gas (water vapour). Because it can change form, it moves from the sea to the air to the land and back again in a circular journey called the **water cycle**. The water cycle is driven by the Sun's heat, which turns liquid water into water vapour. This process is called **evaporation**. When water in the air cools, it turns back into liquid water. This process is called **condensation**. The water then falls from the air as rain or snow.

Salty or fresh?

Sea-water contains large amounts of salts, or minerals*. These are left behind when sea-water evaporates, so water that falls as rain or snow is fresh (non-salty). Land-living plants and animals cannot live on salt water so it is important that there is fresh water on the land.

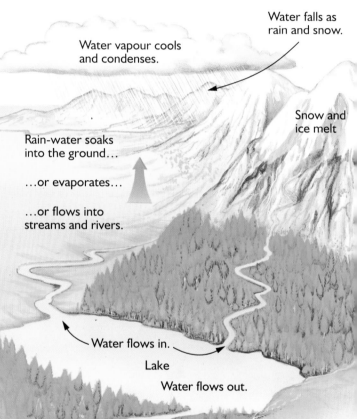

Heat from the Sun makes water evaporate.

Water vapour cools and condenses.

Water falls as rain and snow.

Snow and ice melt

Rain-water soaks into the ground…

…or evaporates…

…or flows into streams and rivers.

When rain falls on land, some of the water settles on the surface and evaporates straight back into the air. Some sinks into the soil and is drawn up by plants, which give it off as vapour through their leaves. The rest of the water flows back to the oceans. It either flows over the land as streams and rivers, or sinks deep down into underground stores called **groundwater**.

Water flows in.

Lake

Water flows out.

Lakes…

Lakes are natural fresh water stores. They form where hollows in the land are filled with water from rivers or streams. Many lakes also have rivers flowing away from them.

Lakes are very important because they fill up when there is heavy rain and prevent flooding. At dry times, they release water and prevent rivers from drying up.

Reservoir

Dam holds back the river.

…and reservoirs

People use huge amounts of fresh water every day, particularly in parts of the world where there is farming and industry. Most of this water comes from big artificial lakes called **reservoirs**. These are made by building dams across rivers to trap the water. In some areas the flow of water is controlled and used to make electricity, called hydro-electric power*.

26 *Hydro-electric power, 75; minerals, 21.*

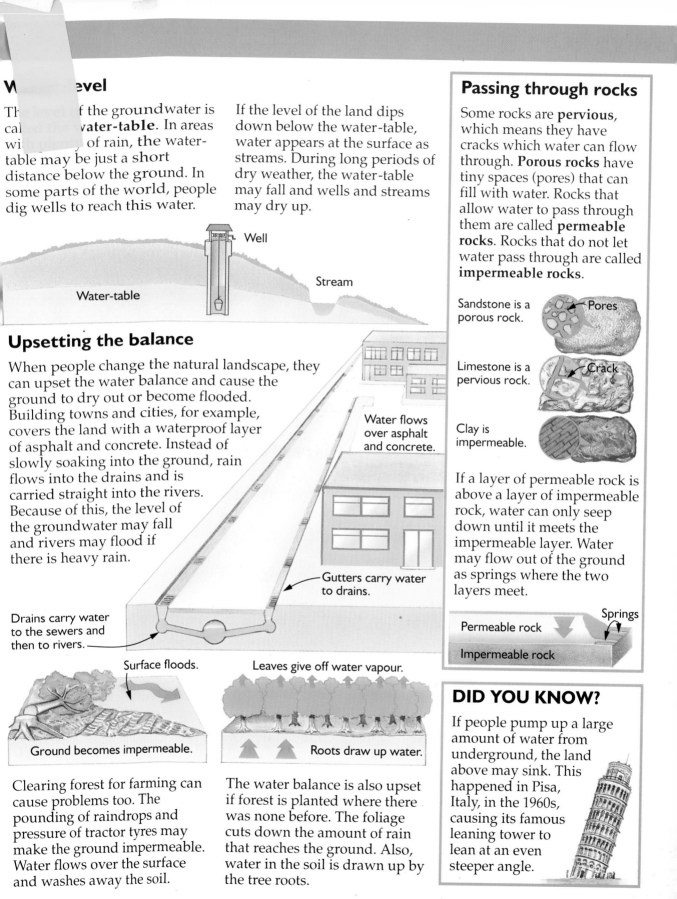

Water level

The level of the groundwater is called the water-table. In areas with plenty of rain, the water-table may be just a short distance below the ground. In some parts of the world, people dig wells to reach this water.

If the level of the land dips down below the water-table, water appears at the surface as streams. During long periods of dry weather, the water-table may fall and wells and streams may dry up.

Well

Stream

Water-table

Upsetting the balance

When people change the natural landscape, they can upset the water balance and cause the ground to dry out or become flooded. Building towns and cities, for example, covers the land with a waterproof layer of asphalt and concrete. Instead of slowly soaking into the ground, rain flows into the drains and is carried straight into the rivers. Because of this, the level of the groundwater may fall and rivers may flood if there is heavy rain.

Water flows over asphalt and concrete.

Gutters carry water to drains.

Drains carry water to the sewers and then to rivers.

Surface floods.

Ground becomes impermeable.

Leaves give off water vapour.

Roots draw up water.

Clearing forest for farming can cause problems too. The pounding of raindrops and pressure of tractor tyres may make the ground impermeable. Water flows over the surface and washes away the soil.

The water balance is also upset if forest is planted where there was none before. The foliage cuts down the amount of rain that reaches the ground. Also, water in the soil is drawn up by the tree roots.

Passing through rocks

Some rocks are pervious, which means they have cracks which water can flow through. Porous rocks have tiny spaces (pores) that can fill with water. Rocks that allow water to pass through them are called permeable rocks. Rocks that do not let water pass through are called impermeable rocks.

Sandstone is a porous rock.

Pores

Limestone is a pervious rock.

Crack

Clay is impermeable.

If a layer of permeable rock is above a layer of impermeable rock, water can only seep down until it meets the impermeable layer. Water may flow out of the ground as springs where the two layers meet.

Springs

Permeable rock

Impermeable rock

DID YOU KNOW?

If people pump up a large amount of water from underground, the land above may sink. This happened in Pisa, Italy, in the 1960s, causing its famous leaning tower to lean at an even steeper angle.

Rivers

As rivers flow over the land they do several important things. They wear away, or **erode**, the rock, creating channels. They then carry the rock particles (their load) to the oceans. This is called **transportation**.

For a river to erode its channel and transport rock particles, or sediment, it needs energy. The faster a river flows, the more energy it has. Rivers flow fastest down steep, narrow, smooth channels. If the channel levels out, widens, or the river-bed becomes coarse, the river slows down and loses energy. The river can no longer transport all its load so it leaves sediment on the river-bed. This process is called **deposition**.

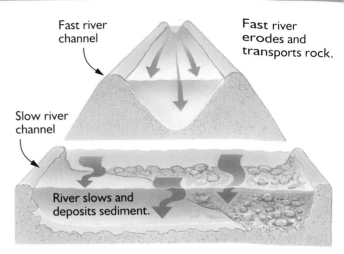

Fast river channel

Fast river erodes and transports rock.

Slow river channel

River slows and deposits sediment.

How does erosion happen?

Rivers erode their channels in several ways. The pressure of water forces into cracks, or joints, in the rock, breaking pieces away. As these are swept along, they chip away more rock. The loose rocks also collide with, and erode, each other. Some rocks dissolve in the water too.

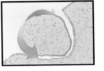
Pressure forces air into joints.

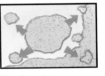
Rocks chip away the channel.

Water dissolves some rocks.

Following a river

Rivers begin high up in hills and mountains and flow down until they eventually meet the oceans. The upper part is steep and the river cuts a deep V-shaped channel. Further towards the sea, the slope is more gentle and the river has a wider channel.

In the lower areas, the river forms bends called **meanders**. Water on the outer edge of the bend has further to travel than water flowing on the inside so it speeds up and has more energy for erosion and transportation. Water flowing on the inside of the bend slows down so deposition happens here.

Over time, the meanders extend further and further, creating a wide, flat valley called a **flood plain**. Where meanders loop back on each other very tightly, the neck separating two loops may be completely eroded and the river may create a new, straight channel. The old loop that is left alongside is called an **ox-bow lake**.

River loops back very tightly.

Narrow neck of land is eroded.

Sediment seals off ox-bow lake.

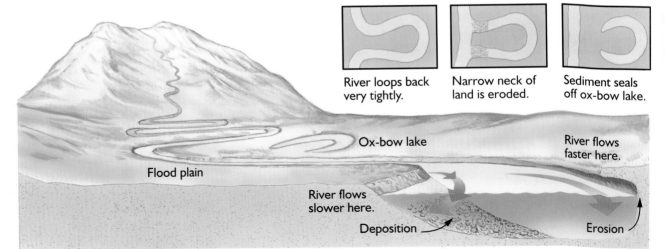

Ox-bow lake

River flows faster here.

Flood plain

River flows slower here.

Deposition

Erosion

Waterfalls and rapids

Waterfalls form where a river-bed crosses from hard rock to softer rock. The river wears down the softer rock and creates a step. The falling water erodes a hollow at the base, called a **plunge pool**.

Spray from the waterfall may under-cut the step and eventually cause it to collapse. Over time, the waterfall may cut back into the hard rock, leaving a steep valley called a **gorge**. Niagara Falls on the Canada/USA border, for example, is cutting into the rock at a rate of 1m (3.3ft) a year and has cut a gorge 11km (6.8 miles) long.

If a river-bed has alternate bands of hard and soft rock, the river may erode it into a series of ledges. This makes the river flow irregularly. Stretches of river where this has happened are called **rapids** or **cataracts**.

Waterfall cutting back.

Side of the gorge

Hard rock

Spray under-cuts here.

Rapids

Layers of hard rock   Softer rock

Plunge pool

Deltas

Deposition often happens where a river channel enters the still water of a lake or the sea. If sediment is deposited faster than it is carried away, it builds up and forms a raised area called a **delta**. As the river flows across the delta, it splits into lots of channels. The most famous deltas are the Nile delta in Egypt and the Mississippi delta in the USA.

Delta

River basins

Rivers are fed by a network of streams called **tributaries**. The area of land that they drain is called a **drainage basin**. Seen from above, river networks make recognizable patterns.

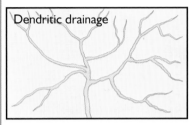

Dendritic drainage

Dendritic patterns, where the river is like a tree trunk with branches, form where the landscape is made up of only one type of rock.

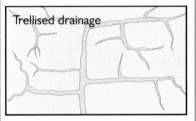

Trellised drainage

Trellised patterns, where the tributaries flow in a rectangular network, form if there are strips of different types of rock. Streams flow along the weak areas where the rocks join.

Radial drainage

Radial drainage, where the streams flow away from a central point, happens where rocks have been lifted up into a dome.

Coasts

The coast, where the land meets the sea, is constantly being shaped by the in and out motion of the waves. Over many years, the action of the waves can produce some spectacular features.

There are two types of waves. **Destructive waves** erode the coast. They are tall and frequent and form in stormy weather. They crash against the shore and carry sand, pebbles and other beach material out to sea.

Constructive waves build up the coast. They have a gentle lapping motion and form in calm weather. They carry beach material on to the shore and leave deposits of sand and pebbles behind.

Destructive waves

Beach material carried out to sea.

Constructive waves

Beach material carried on to the shore.

Eating away the coast

Waves erode soft rocks faster than hard ones so a coastline made up of various different types of rock wears away unevenly. The softer rocks are eaten away into curved bays, whereas more resistant rocks jut out as cliffs and headlands.

Weak points in cliffs, such as joints or cracks, erode faster than the surrounding rock. The sea carves out these areas into caves. Sea-spray may eat out a hole at the top of the cave, called a **blowhole**. Where waves attack a headland, caves may form on both sides. After many years, the two caves meet and an **arch** forms.

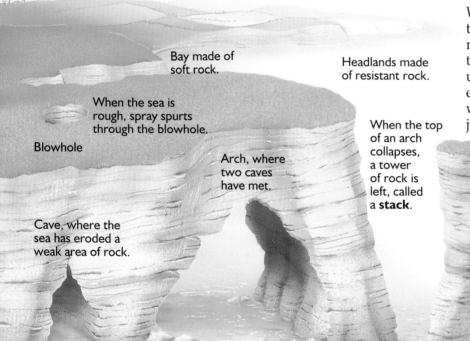

Bay made of soft rock.

When the sea is rough, spray spurts through the blowhole.

Blowhole

Cave, where the sea has eroded a weak area of rock.

Arch, where two caves have met.

Headlands made of resistant rock.

When the top of an arch collapses, a tower of rock is left, called a **stack**.

Crumbling cliffs

Cliffs erode fastest at the base because this area is constantly attacked by the sea. Waves attack the cliff base by hurling rocks at it, chipping away the rock. The surging water also forces air into joints and breaks the rock apart. The sea dissolves some rocks too, such as chalk and limestone.

Collapsing cliff-face

Notch eroded by the sea.

Cliff used to come to here.

Wave-cut platform

Over time, the waves erode a notch at the foot of the cliff and eventually the cliff-face crumbles and collapses.

The cliff gradually crumbles back and back. A flat area of rock is left at the base, called a **wave-cut platform**.

Drifting sands

Waves can move beach material along the shore. They do this by a process called **longshore drift**. Longshore drift happens in places where the wind blows waves in at an angle to the shore. The water does not run back the way it came but flows away straight down the beach, so the waves go in and out in a zig-zag pattern. Sand and pebbles picked up by the waves zig-zag their way along the shore too.

In places where the wind blows from the same direction most of the time, beach material may be carried huge distances by longshore drift. Waves continue to carry sand and pebbles along the shore until the angle of the coast changes, at a bay or the mouth of a river, for example. At this point, the sea deepens and this makes the waves move more slowly. They have less energy for carrying beach material, so they let it fall on to the seabed. The beach material may eventually pile so high that it rises above the level of the sea to form some of the features shown in the picture below.

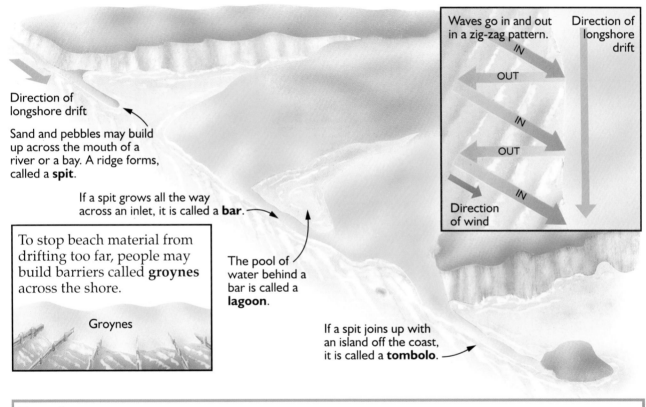

Direction of longshore drift

Sand and pebbles may build up across the mouth of a river or a bay. A ridge forms, called a **spit**.

If a spit grows all the way across an inlet, it is called a **bar**.

To stop beach material from drifting too far, people may build barriers called **groynes** across the shore.

Groynes

The pool of water behind a bar is called a **lagoon**.

If a spit joins up with an island off the coast, it is called a **tombolo**.

Waves go in and out in a zig-zag pattern.

Direction of longshore drift

IN
OUT
IN
OUT
IN

Direction of wind

Beaches

Sand blown on to the land at low tide may form **dune**s at the back of the beach.

Storm ridge

Medium-sized stones

Beaches form from stones and sand washed up by the sea. Bigger stones are thrown to the back of the beach at high tide and the smaller ones are washed down the slope by the outward flow, or **backwash**.

At the very back of the beach there may be a ridge of large boulders that were thrown there by a storm.

The slope of the beach becomes steeper, the bigger the material it is made of.

Pebbles

Coarse sand

Fine sand

Glaciers

Ice covers 10% of the Earth's land surface. Nearly all of it is found in Greenland and Antarctica, near the North and South Poles. The rest is in small areas on high mountains.

In the history of the Earth, there have been long periods of time, called **ice ages**, when the climate was so cold that much more of the land was covered in ice sheets. The last ice age began 2 million years ago and ended only 10,000 years ago, though there were times in between when the ice in some areas melted. One day, there may be another ice age. This map shows where ice covered the Earth during the last ice age and where ice can be found today.

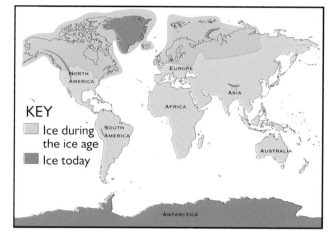

KEY
- Ice during the ice age
- Ice today

Flowing ice

In places where it is always cold and shaded from sunshine, layers of snow become packed into hard, strong ice. If this ice is under pressure or if gravity* pulls it, it slowly flows over the land. Flowing ice is called a **glacier**.

The higher part of a glacier is called the **accumulation zone**. This is where new layers of snow fall and become glacial ice. At the lower end of the glacier is the **ablation zone**, where the ice melts into water, called **meltwater**. As a glacier flows downhill, the ice may stretch and crack into deep openings called **crevasses**.

Most glaciers are less than 2km (1.2 miles) long. However, some are much longer. The Vatnajokul ice cap in Iceland is over 100km (62 miles) long.

Fresh snow and ice

Accumulation zone

Crevasses

Pieces of rock are plucked from the rock surface.

Debris scratches the rocks beneath it.

Ablation zone

Meltwater carries debris away.

Long scratches show that rock has been eroded by a glacier.

Glaciers erode the rock as they move over it. The bottom layer of the glacier freezes around joints and cracks in the rock and then plucks off pieces of rock as the glacier moves along. These pieces of rock are called **debris**. As the glacier moves forward, debris scratches the rock beneath it, and removes a powdery layer from the rock surface. This process is called **abrasion**. It causes the rock surface to look smooth and polished, with long scratches. Eventually, the meltwater carries away the debris and deposits it in another area as thick layers of boulders and clay, called **moraine** or **till**. Most of Denmark is made of this.

*Gravity, 15.

Looking at the landscape

Over many centuries, glaciers carve easily-recognized shapes in the land. For example, when ice collects in a mountain hollow, it may eventually erode the rock and form a deep basin, called a **cirque**, **corrie** or **cwm**. If a mountain has several cirques, a sharp pyramid-shaped peak is formed, like that of the Matterhorn in Switzerland.

Ice from several cirques may flow into a nearby valley, forming a valley glacier. It erodes the sides and bottom into a **U-shaped valley**. Smaller valleys, called **hanging valleys**, which were not cut by a glacier, may be left high above the main valley.

Pyramid-shaped peak

Cirques

Hanging valley

U-shaped valley

Ridge of moraine

Fjord

When a glacier melts, it leaves behind ridges of moraine. Moraine also forms low, long hills called **drumlins**, which may occur in groups.

In Norway and Alaska, there are deep channels cut into the coastline, which slope very steeply from the land down into the sea. These channels, called **fjords**, were carved out by glaciers. When the glaciers melted and sea-levels rose, the fjords were flooded.

Ice hazards

Ice and snow may cause problems for people who live nearby. If a glacier blocks a valley, water may build up. Eventually it breaks through the ice and pours downhill, flooding any villages below.

Most glaciers move only very slowly. However, a glacier may suddenly surge forward very quickly and swallow everything in its path. Earth tremors can cause surges to happen.

In some areas, vibrations from traffic, skiers or earth tremors can make ice and snow fall in an avalanche from the mountains. People plant trees or build fences above the villages to catch the snow.

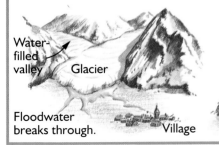

Water-filled valley   Glacier

Floodwater breaks through.   Village

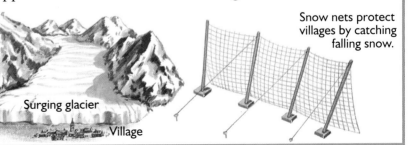

Surging glacier   Village

Snow nets protect villages by catching falling snow.

What makes weather happen?

The atmosphere is constantly moving. As it circulates around the surface of the Earth, movements and changes in the lower layer (the troposphere*) cause different types of weather.

Air moves because of changes in **atmospheric pressure**. This is the push of the atmosphere against the Earth's surface. It is caused by gravity*, which exerts a pull on every particle of air. When air is warmed, it rises, causing low pressure (the particles are further apart). When air is cooled, it sinks, causing high pressure (the particles are closer together). The temperature of the Earth's surface varies a great deal – between the land and sea*, for example – so the air is warmed in some areas and cooled in others.

The atmosphere is always trying to be the same pressure all the way around the Earth, so if pressure is low in one area, air blows in from where the pressure is higher. This air movement is the wind.

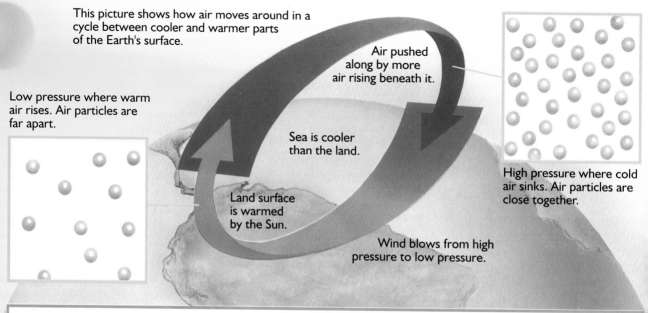

This picture shows how air moves around in a cycle between cooler and warmer parts of the Earth's surface.

Low pressure where warm air rises. Air particles are far apart.

Air pushed along by more air rising beneath it.

Sea is cooler than the land.

Land surface is warmed by the Sun.

High pressure where cold air sinks. Air particles are close together.

Wind blows from high pressure to low pressure.

Global winds

At certain latitudes* on the Earth, there are belts of high pressure and low pressure. Atmospheric pressure is low around the Equator, for example, because the Earth's surface is very hot there.

Strong global winds called **Westerlies** and **Trade Winds** blow from the high pressure belts to the low pressure belts. They do not blow directly north-south between the pressure belts, however. This is because the Earth's spin causes global winds to swing to the side.

This diagram shows the general pattern of world winds. Other factors besides air pressure affect wind direction so this pattern varies in detail.

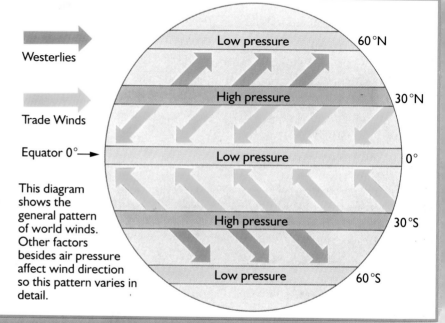

Westerlies

Trade Winds

Equator 0°→

Low pressure — 60°N
High pressure — 30°N
Low pressure — 0°
High pressure — 30°S
Low pressure — 60°S

*Gravity, 15; land and sea temperatures, 39; latitude, 8; troposphere, 15.

What makes it rain?

The atmosphere contains water vapour*. When air rises into the higher, colder atmosphere, the water vapour cools and condenses* into tiny droplets of liquid water. You can see these droplets as clouds. The height where the temperature of the atmosphere is low enough to turn water vapour into droplets of liquid water is called the **dew point**.

As it rises, water vapour cools and condenses. Clouds are made of tiny droplets of water.

Dew point

When air blows inland from the ocean, moist air is forced to rise.

Clouds and rain where moist air cools.

Wet air

The amount of water vapour in the air is called **humidity**. In some hot countries, humidity is very high because the water vapour is not cooled enough to condense.

Air can only hold so much water vapour though. When it is full (saturated), evaporation* stops and everything feels damp.

As more water vapour cools and condenses, droplets in the clouds grow bigger. The droplets become heavy and eventually fall to earth as rain. When water falls from the air as a liquid such as rain or dew, or as a solid such as snow or hail, it is called **precipitation**.

There is often rain in hilly, coastal areas where the wind blows inland from the ocean. This is because ocean wind contains lots of water vapour. When it reaches the land, the air is forced to rise. It cools and the water vapour condenses and falls as rain.

Types of precipitation

When the temperature is very low, water vapour turns into tiny ice crystals and forms snowflakes.

Snow may melt and turn to rain as it falls to earth. Sleet is a mixture of partly melted snow and rain.

Raindrops may freeze within clouds and form hailstones. Hailstones are made up of lots of layers of ice.

Dew settles when warm, moist air passes over cold land and the water vapour condenses around the land surface.

Snowflake made of ice crystals.

Sleet

Cross-section of a hailstone.

Dew drops

DID YOU KNOW?

Sailors out at sea have always been able to tell if land is on the horizon because of the tell-tale clouds that form along the coastline.

*Condensation, evaporation, 26; water vapour, 24.

Weather watching

In many parts of the world the weather changes from day to day. People called meteorologists study weather so they can work out what it might do next. To record weather, they need instruments that measure heat, moisture and atmospheric pressure* because weather is a mixture of all these things.

Rain gauge

Precipitation* (rain, sleet, snow or hail) is measured with a rain gauge. It is collected at ground level and transferred to a measuring cylinder.

A thermometer is a device used to measure heat. It contains mercury or alcohol, which expands and moves up the tube when it is warmed. The liquid rises further up the tube, the hotter it becomes.

Thermometer

Aneroid barometer

A barometer measures air pressure. One type, called an aneroid barometer, has a dial and a needle, which moves around when the air pressure changes. It measures air pressure in hectopascals (hPa) or in millibars (mb).

Humidity* is measured by wet and dry bulb thermometers. Wet muslin covers one bulb. When there is not much moisture in the air, water evaporates* from the muslin. Evaporation cools the bulb so the temperature falls below that of the dry bulb thermometer. The temperature difference shows how humid it is.

Wet and dry bulb thermometer

Look at temperature difference to work out humidity.

Evaporation cools the wet bulb.

Wet bulb   Dry bulb

A weather vane shows wind direction. An arrow points towards where the wind is coming from.

An anemometer measures how fast the wind is blowing. Cups catch the wind and are pushed around. A meter records how quickly they spin.

Weather vane

N   E
W   S

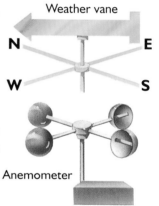

Anemometer

Weather charts

Meteorologists work at weather stations. They collect data about the weather and plot it on charts. On the charts, lines called **isobars** join up places with the same atmospheric pressure. Arrows show which way the wind is blowing. Lines, or feathers, on the end show wind speed in knots. Half a feather stands for five knots, a whole feather stands for ten knots. Symbols on the charts show how much cloud cover there is.

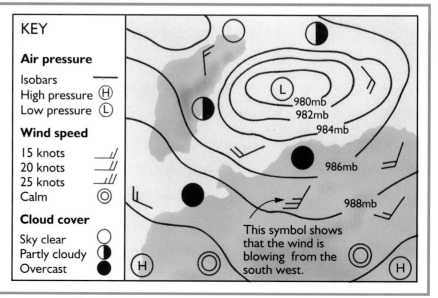

KEY

Air pressure

Isobars —
High pressure Ⓗ
Low pressure Ⓛ

Wind speed

15 knots
20 knots
25 knots
Calm ◎

Cloud cover

Sky clear ○
Partly cloudy ◐
Overcast ●

980mb
982mb
984mb
986mb
988mb

This symbol shows that the wind is blowing from the south west.

Fronts and depressions

A **front** is where an area of cold air and an area of warm air meet. A **warm front** is where warm air is moving in to replace cold air. A **cold front** is where cold air is replacing warm air. On weather charts, fronts are shown by lines marking their leading edge. Warm fronts have rounded nobbles along them. Cold fronts have triangles.

If an area of warm air is wedged in an expanse of colder air it is called a **depression**. The cold air pushes underneath the warm air and eventually the warm and cold fronts meet. When this happens it is called an **occluded front**.

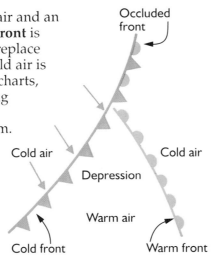

Occluded front

Cold air

Cold air

Depression

Warm air

Cold front

Warm front

Satellite pictures

Satellites out in space take pictures of the Earth. From these, meteorologists can see the pattern and movement of clouds around the world. This helps them to understand how the weather works.

Cloud spotting

It is often possible to work out what the weather will do next by studying the height, shape and colour of the clouds. Clouds form along fronts, so they often signal that a depression is on its way – and this usually means unsettled weather.

There are three main categories of cloud. **Cirrus** clouds are high and wispy, **cumulus** clouds are lower and look like heaps of cotton wool, and **stratus** clouds form in layers. Many clouds are a combination of two types, as shown below.

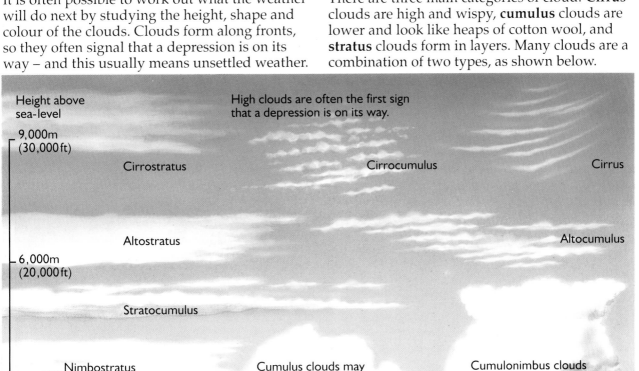

Height above sea-level

High clouds are often the first sign that a depression is on its way.

9,000m (30,000 ft)

Cirrostratus

Cirrocumulus

Cirrus

Altostratus

Altocumulus

6,000m (20,000 ft)

Stratocumulus

Nimbostratus clouds bring rain or snow.

Cumulus clouds may be a sign of fine weather in summer.

Cumulonimbus clouds usually signal thunder, lightning, rain or snow.

2,000m (6,500 ft)

37

Hot and cold places

In some areas of the world, the average weather, or **climate**, is much hotter than in other areas. The main reason for this is to do with the area's latitude*. Areas near the Equator (low latitudes) have a hot climate because the Sun rises high overhead and its rays strike the Earth almost at right angles. The land and sea become very warm and pass on heat to the air. Passing on heat like this is called **radiation**.

Areas near the Poles (high latitudes) are cold because the Sun stays low in the sky and its rays spread out over a much wider area. The land and sea are hardly warmed so they have very little heat to radiate.

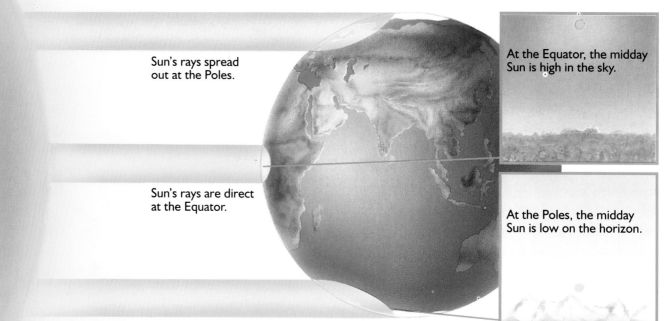

Sun's rays spread out at the Poles.

Sun's rays are direct at the Equator.

At the Equator, the midday Sun is high in the sky.

At the Poles, the midday Sun is low on the horizon.

Daylight hours

In every part of the world except the Equator, the length of day and night varies depending on the time of year. When days are long* the land and sea have a long time to warm up so they have more heat to radiate. This makes the climate warmer. At night, the Earth's surface is turned away from the Sun's rays so it cools down. Therefore, when the nights are long, the climate becomes colder.

High places

The temperature of the air around you depends partly on the atmospheric pressure*. If atmospheric pressure is low, there are fewer particles of air close to the Earth's surface to trap heat, so the air stays cold.

Atmospheric pressure is low in high, mountainous areas, where gravity* is weaker. This is why mountainous areas are cold and snowy – even those close to the Equator.

Fewer molecules, so air stays cool.

More molecules to trap heat.

DID YOU KNOW?

The hottest place on Earth is Dalol in Ethiopia. The average temperature there is 34°C (94°F). The coldest place on Earth is Polus Nedostupnosti in Antarctica, where the average temperature is -58°C (-72°F).

Dalol

Polus Nedostupnosti

Land and sea temperatures

Places close to the sea have a milder climate than places a long way inland. Oceans heat up more slowly than land because their shiny surface reflects the Sun's rays, but they stay warm longer. Places near the coast are cooled by the sea in summer and warmed by the sea in winter. The central parts of continents have much hotter summers and colder winters.

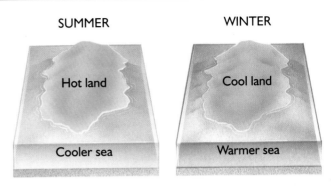

SUMMER
Hot land
Cooler sea

WINTER
Cool land
Warmer sea

Winds and ocean currents*

Warm and cold winds blowing around the world also influence climate. The temperature of the wind depends on where it has blown from. Winds blowing from the Tropics to higher latitudes are warm because they drag currents of warm tropical water with them. The ocean's heat makes the wind warm too. Winds blowing from the Poles are very cold because they are chilled by the cold ocean currents beneath them. This map shows the main ocean currents.

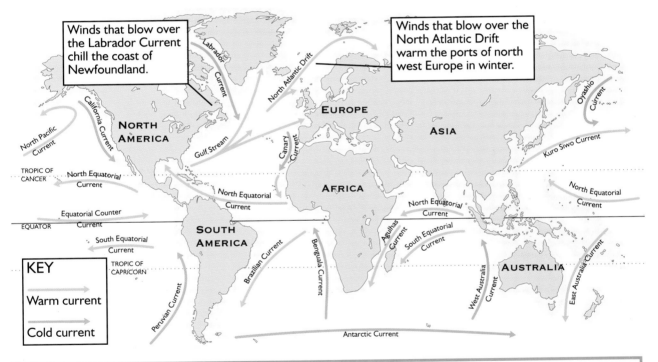

Winds that blow over the Labrador Current chill the coast of Newfoundland.

Winds that blow over the North Atlantic Drift warm the ports of north west Europe in winter.

KEY

→ Warm current

→ Cold current

Cloud cover

Clouds make places cooler during the day because they block some of the Sun's rays. At night they trap in heat and keep the air warm. Blocking out or trapping in heat is called **insulation**. Some areas, such as equatorial regions*, are always cloudy. Days would be much hotter and nights much colder there if the sky was clear.

Clouds keep heat out during the day.

Clouds trap heat in at night.

*Currents, 25; equatorial regions, 42.

Extreme weather

Sometimes weather can behave in such extreme or violent ways that it makes news headlines. Violent weather can cause a lot of damage to land and buildings, and even kill people.

Thunderstorms

Thunderstorms are also called **electrical storms**. They happen when raindrops and hailstones crash into each other and create an electrical charge in a cloud. The electricity jumps through the air to land, or to other clouds nearby. The air becomes very hot and expands quickly, which causes a bang like an explosion (thunder) and a flash (lightning).

Light travels faster than sound so you see the lightning before you hear the thunder. To work out how far away the centre of a storm is, count the seconds between when you see the lightning and when you hear the thunder. Divide the number of seconds by three to work out how far away the storm is in kilometres or divide the number by five to work it out in miles.

You see sheet lightning if cloud blocks your view.

You see forked lightning if the path of the electricity is visible.

Revolving storms

Hurricanes, **typhoons** and **cyclones** are all names for tropical revolving storms. These develop when air rises over the warm, tropical seas and starts spinning. No one is sure what sets it off. Most revolving storms develop in the Pacific Ocean and blow over the Philippines, Hong Kong, China and Japan. They also affect northern Australia and the southern USA.

Revolving storms are usually about 500km (310 miles) across and travel at about 15kmph (9mph). The centre of the storm, called the **eye**, is calm but fast winds circle around it. At the edge of the storm, the wind may blow at speeds of over 120kmph (75mph) and can blow down buildings. There is also torrential rain, which may cause flooding.

Satellites out in space can detect the spiral cloud pattern of a revolving storm before it reaches land. Forecasters are able to send out warnings so that people can be prepared.

Air spirals up in the centre.

This picture shows a cross-section of a revolving storm.

Direction of wind

Wind blows fastest at the outer edge of the storm.

The eye of the storm is calm.

Tornadoes and water-spouts

A **tornado** is a spinning column of air, usually about 0.5km (0.3 miles) wide. There is very low atmospheric pressure* at its centre and this causes the tornado to suck things up off the ground as it passes.

Tornadoes travel at speeds of around 400kmph (248mph). They usually die out after about 20km (12.5 miles).

Tornadoes are most common in Australia and the USA, where they are sometimes called twisters. They form during summer storms.

Water-spouts are similar to tornadoes but they form over the sea. The centre of the storm sucks up sea water and spray, so a long funnel of mist and cloud forms between the sea and the sky.

Tornado

Low pressure in the centre of the tornado sucks things up off the ground.

High winds

When wind blows at more than 63kmph (40mph) it is called a **gale**. Gales may develop when winds blow across oceans or large flat areas of land. In coastal areas, gales can whip up the waves and cause floods. The salt water can make land near the coast impossible to farm for several years.

Strong winds can cause giant waves.

Wind can also reach gale force if it is channelled through a valley or between tall buildings. This is called the **funnel effect**.

Funnel effect

DID YOU KNOW?

Tornadoes and water-spouts are capable of sucking up small creatures from the ground or sea. In one case, hundreds of pink frogs which had been sucked up in the Sahara, Africa, fell back to earth over a thousand miles away, in the UK.

Too little rain

In most parts of the world, it is possible to forecast how much rain there will be each month. If there is a lot less rain than expected, the conditions are classed as **drought**.

In countries where there is usually plenty of rain, drought does not affect people very much. They just have to use less water in their homes and gardens until it is over.

Drought can be disastrous, though, in areas of the world where rainfall is unreliable, such as India, parts of Africa and central Australia. If there is no rain, crops do not grow and there is no pasture for sheep and cattle.

Equatorial regions

Most places near to the Equator have an equatorial climate. The Sun's rays are very direct there so the climate is hot. It is also very rainy because the Sun's heat makes lots of water evaporate*. Warm, humid air rises and cools to form huge storm clouds.

The equatorial regions are the only areas of the world where the seasons* do not change.

Mountainous areas have a cooler climate.

Tropic of Cancer

Equator

Tropic of Capricorn

Equatorial regions

The rainforests

Most of the equatorial region is covered in thick forest, called **equatorial rainforest**. Hundreds of types of hardwood trees grow there, such as mahogany, rosewood and ebony.

The rainforest is so dense that the trees have to fight for sunlight. They grow very tall and spread out their upper branches to catch more light. Their tops form a thick layer of foliage called a **canopy**, which cuts out sunlight to the forest floor. Some giant trees, called **emergent trees**, tower above the canopy.

Beneath the canopy the rainforest is damp and gloomy. Plants that grow on the forest floor have broad, flat leaves to catch as much sunlight as possible. The leaves have a waxy surface and a point at the tip, called a **drip tip**, to let rain run off more easily.

At ground level there is a mass of rotting vegetation and fungus. In clearings, where trees have fallen, new trees shoot up in a race to claim a share of the sunlight. The one that grows fastest will replace the tree that has fallen. Climbing plants called **lianas** attach themselves to the young trees and grow with them up to the sunlight.

The canopy is 7m (23ft) thick in places.

Emergent tree

Some trees produce brightly coloured flowers at their crowns.

Broad, waxy leaves

Liana

Drip tip

Tall trees need strong supporting trunks. Some grow flared buttresses to help hold them up.

42   *Evaporation, 26; seasons, 7.

Forest creatures

Millions of different types of creatures live in the equatorial rainforests as there is plenty of food, water and warmth.

Eagle

Birds of prey live in the emergent trees. From there they have a clear view over their hunting ground.

Creatures that live in the canopy, such as those below, feed on fruit, nuts, flowers, leaves and bark.

Toucan

Fruit bat

Parrot

Animals that live among the branches need to be able to move easily from tree to tree.

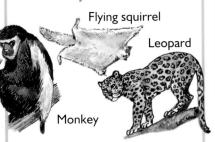

Flying squirrel

Leopard

Monkey

Small creatures live on the forest floor. The tangled vegetation makes it hard for large animals to move about.

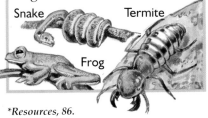

Snake

Termite

Frog

People of the rainforests

Various tribes live in the rainforests, such as the Pygmies of Zaire, Africa, and the Amazonian Indians of South America. They are **nomads**, which means they move from place to place. Some are **hunter-gatherers**, which means they live on whatever they find or catch in the forest.

Rainforest people are small – usually no more than 140cm (4½ft) tall. They can move through the forest easily.

Forest dwellers make clothing from materials around them. This Pygmy is wearing a loincloth of softened bark.

Hunter-gatherers hunt animals and gather other food such as nuts, fruit and honey.

Some rainforest people make small clearings to grow some of their own food. They burn the chopped down trees and spread the ashes, which make the soil fertile for a while. When the fertility has been used up, the people move to a new patch. This way of farming is called **slash and burn**.

Shelters are covered with waxy leaves to keep out the rain.

Smoke from fires drives away insects.

Shrinking forests

Cities

Mining

Roads

Farming

Huge areas of rainforest are cleared each year. A lot of the land is used for farming commercial crops such as palm oil, coffee, cocoa and rubber. Forest is also cleared to build roads and cities, and to mine minerals such as copper, zinc and diamonds. Some wood is sold abroad for furniture-making and building. Some goes to industries to be made into charcoal for fuel. Many people worry that clearing large areas of rainforest will destroy important resources*.

Savanna regions

Areas a few degrees north and south of the Equator have a climate which is usually very dry. At certain times of the year, though, they become very hot and have torrential rain. These areas of the world are called the savanna regions. They are named after the Savanna in Africa, which is the largest region with this type of climate.

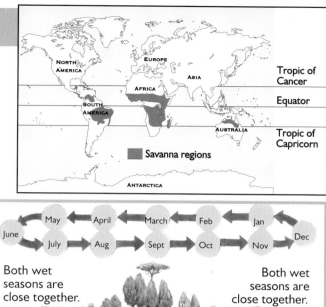
Savanna regions

When the rain comes

The savanna regions are within the Tropics, where the Sun is directly overhead twice each year. It is hotter at these times of the year so more water evaporates* and this causes heavy rain. In areas of savanna closest to the Equator, the Sun is directly overhead at opposite times of the year (around March and September) so the rainy seasons are several months apart. In areas of savanna furthest from the Equator, both rainy seasons are so close together that they merge into one.

Both wet seasons are close together.

Both wet seasons are close together.

Savanna   Equatorial   Savanna

Tropic of Cancer   Equator   Tropic of Capricorn

This picture shows where the Sun is most direct, month by month.

What grows in the savanna?

Conditions in the savanna are harsh. The soil contains few nutrients, dries out during the dry season and becomes boggy during the wet season. Also, there are often fires at the end of the dry season.

Grasses are very tough and can grow easily in savanna conditions. Thousands of different types grow there. For trees to survive, though, they need certain features to protect them against drought and fire.

One type of tree, called the baobab tree, has developed a thick, fireproof trunk, which stores water like a sponge. Its long roots draw water from deep underground. Other trees, such as acacia trees, have broad, flat crowns to shade the lower leaves and prevent them from drying out.

Broad crown shades lower leaves.

Baobab tree

Acacia tree

Thick trunk stores water.

Fires spread easily through the dry grass.

*Evaporation, 26.

Savanna wildlife

Many savanna areas have been used for farming cattle and the natural wildlife has gone. In the African Savanna, though, there are huge national parks where wild animals still live.

Savanna animals have to be able to survive the drought. Large plant-eaters (herbivores) such as giraffes, zebras, wildebeest, elephants and rhinos can travel huge distances so, when one area becomes too dry, they wander to where there is rain and vegetation. Meat-eaters (carnivores), such as lions, cheetahs and hyenas prey on the roaming herds. Animals too small to travel to water may sleep through the dry season. This is called aestivation. Many small creatures live underground and only come out after sunset when it is cooler.

Herds of wildebeest may travel huge distances in search of water and vegetation.

Savanna people

Many tribes live in the African Savanna. The Fulani tribe, for example, are nomads*. They keep cattle, sheep and goats and travel the land in search of water and fresh pasture.

The Fulani live mainly on milk from their herds. They also sell leather and milk to buy cereals. In the rainy season they make shelters from branches and leather. In the dry season they sleep in the open air.

Bedding and mats are made out of dry grasses.

Shelters are made out of branches and hides.

Commercial farming

Higher areas of the African Savanna are cooler than the lower regions so they have more rain. The soil has more moisture and fertility so commercial crops such as tea and coffee may be grown on the hillsides there.

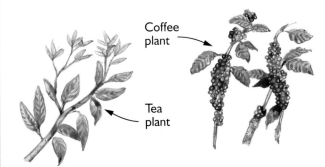

Coffee plant

Tea plant

The Brazilian and Australian savanna regions also have fairly regular rain. This makes them ideal for cattle farming. Over the past century, European settlers have made large areas into cattle ranches. Much of the beef reared there is sold to European countries.

*Nomads, 43.

Tropical deserts

The world's tropical deserts are between about 15° and 30° north and south of the Equator. Air that rose at the Equator sinks here, causing high atmospheric pressure*. The air becomes warm as it nears the Earth's surface, so it can hold lots of water vapour without it condensing*. Because of this, clouds hardly ever form within these regions and rain is very rare.

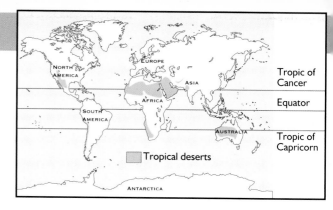

Desert landscapes

All desert landscapes are very dry. The landscape usually has little vegetation because of lack of rain.

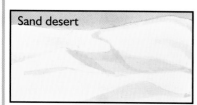

Sand desert

About 25% of the world's deserts are made up of sand, which has been blown from rock faces. It forms hills called **dunes**. The Sahara in Africa is a sandy desert.

Stony desert

Some deserts are made up of bare stone. There is stony desert in Algeria and Libya, for example.

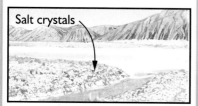

Salt crystals

In some places, such as Salt Lake City in the USA, large lakes have dried up, leaving a layer of salt crystals.

Desert conditions

The tropical deserts are the hottest places on Earth. With no clouds to block the Sun's rays, the ground becomes baking hot. Nights can be very cold, though, and even frosty in winter, because cloudless skies let heat escape.

Strong Trade Winds* blow across the deserts. In sandy deserts, the wind sweeps up fine sand and causes dust storms. As sand is blown along, it erodes rocks in its path. Over many years the rocks may be sand-blasted into weird, sculptural shapes.

Although desert rain is rare, it is usually heavy. Wide rivers form, which carry lots of rock particles (sediment). This erodes rocks and eats out deep canyons. The rivers soon dry up, leaving dry courses called **wadis**.

Deep canyon eroded by floodwater

Rock eroded by the desert wind

DID YOU KNOW?

Some parts of the Atacama Desert in South America, have had no rain for several hundred years.

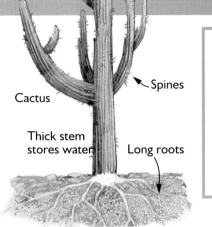

Plant life

Desert plants have to survive with very little rain. Some, such as cacti, store water in their stems, leaves or roots. These are called **succulent plants**. Many plants have spines instead of leaves because spines allow less moisture to escape. Many desert plants have long roots for finding water.

Cactus

Spines

Thick stem stores water

Long roots

Flowering deserts

Some desert plants only grow when it rains. Their seeds may lie in the ground for years, just waiting. When rain comes, they grow, flower and die within a few days.

Desert creatures

Desert creatures need to keep their bodies as cool and moist as possible. Small animals cope by staying in the shade. Some desert creatures have developed particular features and types of behaviour that help them to live more easily in the hot, dry desert conditions.

Carnivores such as this desert fox take in moisture from the blood of their prey.

Many desert animals have long ears, which lose heat easily.

Desert rats stay in moist underground burrows.

Camels can close their nostrils partly during dust storms to stop them from breathing in sand.

Termite nests point north-south so only a small area faces the general direction of the Sun.

Long eyelashes protect a camel's eyes from dust storms.

A camel has no fat under its skin so it stays cooler. Instead, fat is stored in its hump.

Wide, padded feet stop camels from sinking into the sand.

Living in the desert

Only 5% of the world's people live in desert areas. Many are nomads*, others live in small fertile areas called **oases**. Oases form around springs or wells where people can settle permanently. In the Sahara and Arabian desert, the date palm is a major oasis crop.

Broad leaves are used for roofs. They are also woven into rope, and used as fuel.

Dates are a nutritious fruit. The ground-up stones are fed to camels.

Trunks are used for building.

Date palm

*Nomads, 43.

Monsoon regions

Monsoons are very heavy rainstorms that blow in from the oceans and affect large land masses in the Tropics. About a quarter of the world's population lives in monsoon areas.

Monsoons only occur during a particular part of the year. In the northern hemisphere, they arrive in June. In the monsoon regions of Australia, they arrive in December.

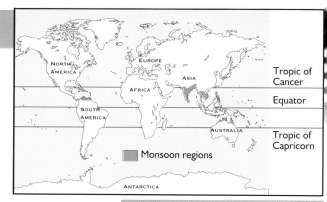

Monsoon seasons

Monsoon areas have three seasons. Before the rains arrive, there is a hot, humid season as the air becomes more moist. The land is dry and bare from months without rain.

During the rainy season (the monsoon), the sky is grey for several weeks. There are thunderstorms almost every day and there is often flooding.

After the monsoon, there is a long, cool, dry season. The sky clears and the floodwater settles. There may be no more rain until the following year.

Rain in the wind

For most of the year, monsoon areas are fairly dry. This is because the atmospheric pressure* is higher over the land than the sea. Wind blows from high pressure to low so dry winds blow from inland towards the sea.

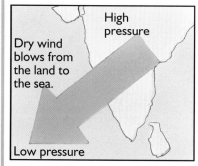

Dry wind blows from the land to the sea.

During the hottest months of the year, the air pressure over the land is lower than over the sea so the wind changes direction and blows inland.

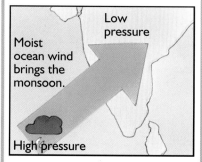

Moist ocean wind brings the monsoon.

The ocean wind has travelled over large areas of warm sea and holds lots of moisture. This falls over the land as torrential, monsoon rain.

*Atmospheric pressure, 34.

Farming

Most monsoon areas have a very dense population, which relies on farming for food. Many areas of natural forest have been chopped down so that the land can be used to grow rice, wheat and millet.

Rice needs lots of water so the seedlings are planted during the monsoon in flooded fields called **paddy fields**. Floodwater is stored in wells and reservoirs to irrigate* crops during drier months.

Tea is also grown in monsoon areas, particularly India and Sri Lanka, which are the world's main tea producers.

Village women plant rice seedlings in flooded paddy fields.

Animal life

Many of Asia's wild animals have almost died out as the natural vegetation has disappeared. They include tigers, leopards, Indian elephants and wild boars. In the wet season, many areas are infested by insects, snakes, frogs and toads.

In northern Australia's monsoon areas, crocodiles live in the river estuaries.

Indian tiger

Too much or too little

It is usually possible to predict when the monsoon will arrive but no one knows how much rain there will be. Some years there is too much and towns and cities are flooded. If there is too little rain, however, crops cannot grow, the cattle die of thirst and the people may starve.

Because people rely on the monsoon rain for their existence, there is great relief and excitement when it arrives. The weeks beforehand are hot and uncomfortable so the rain is refreshing. In some areas, people celebrate the arrival of the monsoon with parties or parades.

Floods can damage people's homes but too little rain may lead to starvation.

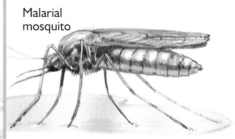

Water diseases

Serious diseases such as cholera and typhoid are common in monsoon areas. The bacteria that cause them breed in water, so during the monsoon floods it is easy for the diseases to spread. Mosquitoes that carry the disease, malaria, also breed in the pools of stale water.

Malarial mosquito

DID YOU KNOW?

At the height of the monsoon season, Cherrapunji in India is the wettest place on Earth. It has an average rainfall of almost 1m (over 3ft) each day.

*Irrigation, 69.

Temperate regions

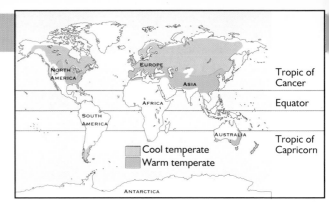

Most places that are between the cold polar regions and the hot Tropics have a temperate climate, which is neither extremely hot nor extremely cold. There are two types of temperate climate. Areas that are further towards the Tropics have a warm temperate climate and areas further towards the Poles have a cool temperate climate.

Temperate seasons

Temperate regions have four seasons: spring, summer, autumn and winter. Cool temperate regions may have frosty winters but summers are mild. Warm temperate regions are closer to the Equator so all the seasons are several degrees hotter. The average temperature in these parts of the world is 27°C (80°F), so the climate is comfortable to live in. Most temperate areas have some rain most months. In winter, cool temperate regions may have snow.

Living in temperate lands

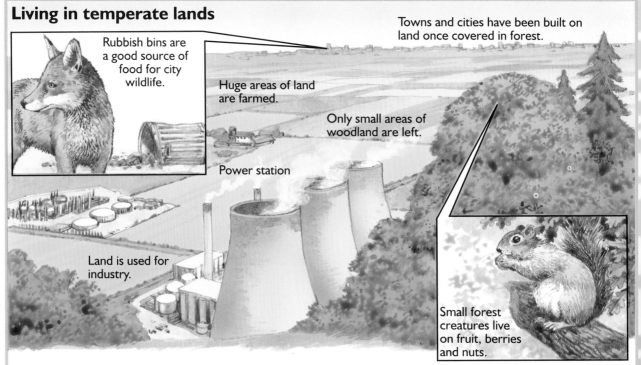

Rubbish bins are a good source of food for city wildlife.

Towns and cities have been built on land once covered in forest.

Huge areas of land are farmed.

Only small areas of woodland are left.

Power station

Land is used for industry.

Small forest creatures live on fruit, berries and nuts.

The temperate climate is ideal for agriculture because the weather is not too hot or too cold and there is regular rain. Huge areas are farmed, such as the Steppes in Russia and Asia and the Prairies in North America, where most of the world's cereals are grown.

Farming has produced wealth, so industries have grown too. As areas have become more developed, natural vegetation such as forests and grasslands have been cleared so that more land can be used for towns and factories.

As land has been farmed or built on, many wild animals have disappeared. For example, herds of bison once grazed on the grasslands and huge numbers of deer and wolves lived in the forests. Now, mainly birds and small rodents such as squirrels are left in the patches of forest that are still standing.

Some temperate creatures have adapted to living in the towns and cities. For example, foxes, many rodents, birds and insects now make their homes among buildings.

Temperate winds

The temperate climate varies between the east and west of a land mass. This is because it is affected by global winds.

Cool temperate regions have Westerly Winds*. The west has more rain than the east because the wind reaches the west coast first, after crossing the ocean. Western areas also have milder winters and cooler summers because the wind is cooled by the ocean in summer and warmed in winter. Inland, the ground becomes very hot in summer and very cold in winter and it heats or cools the wind as it blows to the east.

Warm temperate regions only have Westerly Winds during the winter. In summer, they are affected by Trade Winds*, which blow from east to west. In summer, therefore, these regions have most rain in the east.

This diagram shows an imaginary land mass in the northern hemisphere*.

- ☐ Cool temperate
- ☐ Warm temperate

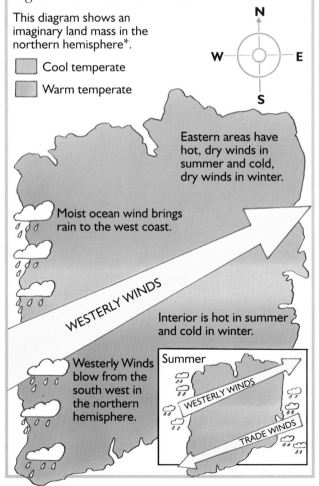

Eastern areas have hot, dry winds in summer and cold, dry winds in winter.

Moist ocean wind brings rain to the west coast.

WESTERLY WINDS

Interior is hot in summer and cold in winter.

Westerly Winds blow from the south west in the northern hemisphere.

Summer
WESTERLY WINDS
TRADE WINDS

Temperate vegetation

Just as the climate varies across the temperate regions, so does the vegetation. Some typical vegetation is shown in the pictures below. The maps, which are of an imaginary land mass in the northern hemisphere, show where each type of vegetation would be found.

In the coldest areas, trees have needle-like leaves because narrow leaves save moisture in winter when water freezes. These trees are called **conifers**. Coniferous forests still exist in Canada, Siberia and Scandinavia.

Conifer

Most of the trees that grow in temperate regions lose their leaves in winter when there is not very much sunlight. Trees that lose their leaves are called **deciduous trees**. Oak, beech, chestnut and maple are examples of deciduous trees.

Deciduous tree

In warm temperate regions, the west normally has more vegetation than the east. This is because the west has rain in winter when it is cool so the moisture stays in the soil. Evergreen oak, cypress and cedar trees grow there.

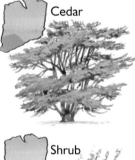

Cedar

The eastern parts of warm temperate regions have most rain in the summer. The heat causes moisture to evaporate* quickly so the soil is dry. Few trees can grow in the dry soil but shrubs can grow easily.

Shrub

In central areas, the climate is too harsh for trees but ideal for grasses. The temperate grasslands are as follows: the Prairies (USA); the Steppes (Russia and Asia); the Veld (South Africa); the Downs (Australia) and the Pampas (South America).

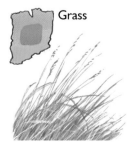

Grass

Polar regions

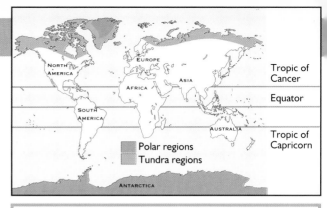

The Sun's rays are weakest at the Poles so they are the coldest parts of the Earth. The region around the North Pole, called the Arctic, is an expanse of frozen ocean. The Antarctic in the south is ice-covered land. These frozen areas are called the **polar ice caps**. The areas of land around the edges of the northern ice cap are called **tundra regions**.

Powerful, icy-cold polar winds blow across Arctic and Antarctic regions throughout the year. Often the wind sweeps up powdery snow from the ground and swirls it around, causing blizzards. Very little new snow or rain falls as it is too cold for moisture to evaporate*.

DID YOU KNOW?

The Antarctic ice cap is 3.7km (2.3 miles) thick in places. If it all melted, the oceans would rise by 55m (180ft).

Life on Antarctica

Very few plants grow on the icy continent of Antarctica so there is no food inland for animals to live on. Therefore, Antarctic animals live in or near the sea. There are many seabirds, such as petrels, albatross, gulls, and terns. Penguins also live on Antarctica.

Penguins are well protected against the cold. Deep feathers trap warmth close to their bodies. Thick skin and a layer of fat give extra insulation. In fact, penguins are so snug that they may over-heat. If they do, they stick out their wings to cool down.

Antarctic laboratory

No one lives permanently in Antarctica so it has not been spoilt. Scientists do tests on the atmosphere there because it is so pure.

Penguins' feathers grow very close together. The tip of each feather curls inwards to trap heat.

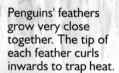

Soft, tufty underfeathers trap warmth close to the penguin's body. Wind and water cannot get through.

Antarctic sea life

The sea around Antarctica is home to dolphins, porpoises, whales, seals and other sea creatures. They have a thick layer of oily fat called blubber to keep them warm.

Humpback whale

Dusky dolphin

These creatures are not to scale.

Blubber protects sea creatures from the icy-cold water.

The tundra regions

The tundra lands around the northern ice cap stay frozen for nine months of the year. In the summer months (May, June, July), only the surface thaws. Deeper ground stays frozen. This frozen layer is called **permafrost**. Melted snow cannot seep through the permafrost so, in summer, the surface of the tundra lands becomes boggy.

When ice crystals in the land melt, the ground shrinks. When the land freezes again, it expands. Thawing and freezing over and over again cause the surface of the tundra to form angular patterns called **polygons**.

Tundra vegetation such as moss, shrubs, and spreading plants called lichens grow close to the ground to avoid the strong winds.

Tundra is boggy in summer.

Polygons

Permafrost

Plants grow close to the ground.

Tundra people

Only a few thousand people live in the tundra regions. The Inuit live in northern Canada, Greenland and Alaska. The Lapps herd reindeer in northern Scandinavia.

Traditionally, the Inuit were hunters and fishermen. They travelled by sledge and built temporary ice shelters called igloos during hunting trips. For warmth, the Inuit wore a double layer of fur clothing. They wore the inner layer with the furry side towards their skin to trap body heat.

Houses built on stilts.

Pipes

Inuit hunter wearing traditional furs.

Snowmobile

Today, hunters may still wear traditional furs but many Inuit dress in modern clothes. Some have motor-powered snowmobiles and homes made of modern materials. Some homes have electricity and telephones. Heated houses have to be built on stilts so that the permafrost does not thaw. If it did, the ground would give way. Water pipes are insulated and run above ground to stop them from freezing.

Arctic animals

Over thousands of years, land animals have spread north and adapted to living in the Arctic.

Polar bears live on the frozen ocean. Long, waterproof fur covers the soles of their paws to help grip the ice.

Musk oxen

Musk oxen have a fine layer of wool under a thick outer coat. They crowd together so water vapour in their breath forms a cloud to trap heat.

Lemming

Small rodents such as lemmings live in snow-tunnels.

Reindeer, also called caribou, travel south in winter. Their huge hoofs do not sink into the boggy ground or soft snow.

Caribou

Many polar creatures have white fur for camouflage. Some tundra animals, such as ermine, go darker in the summer.

Winter coat

Ermine's summer coat

People of the world

Most experts believe that humans probably evolved (developed gradually) in Africa around two or three million years ago. As time went by, they spread out into other parts of Africa and into Asia and Europe. Their physical features slowly adapted to their surroundings and three main groups developed – **Negros**, **Mongolians** and **Caucasians**. Eventually, people arrived in America and Australasia, where the American Indians and the Australasian Aborigines and Maoris developed.

Though it is still possible to recognize the features of the different groups in modern people, pure types no longer exist. Physical features are mixed together as people migrate around the world and inter-marry.

This map shows how humans spread out all over the world.

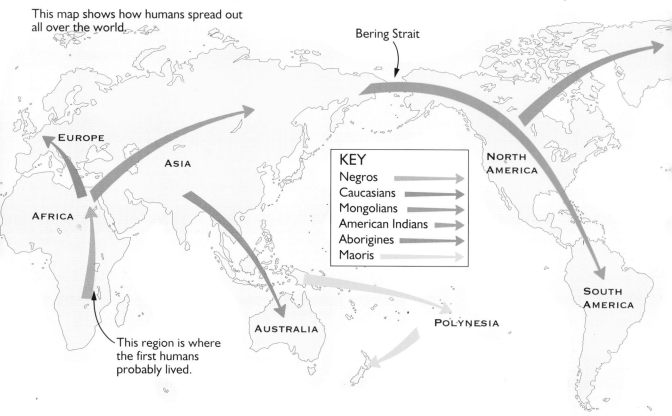

Bering Strait

EUROPE

ASIA

AFRICA

NORTH AMERICA

KEY
Negros
Caucasians
Mongolians
American Indians
Aborigines
Maoris

AUSTRALIA

POLYNESIA

SOUTH AMERICA

This region is where the first humans probably lived.

Negros

Pure Negros evolved in Africa, where it is very hot. Their dark skin and eyes had a lot of pigment for protection against the hot sun. Tightly-curled hair protected their heads from heat. The people of the Sudan, west and central Africa, and the Bantu people are descended from them.

Negro from central Africa

Mongolians

Pure Mongolians came from Asia, where it can be very cold. Their round faces were padded with fat for warmth. Narrow eyes with an extra fold of skin on the eyelids protected them from snow glare and biting winds. The Japanese, Chinese and people of central Asia are their descendants.

Mongolian from China

Caucasians

Caucasian people came from Europe, northern Africa, the Middle East and the Indian sub-continent, where the climate is not as hot as places nearer the Equator. Caucasians had pale skin and eyes because they did not need so much pigment to protect them as those people living in hotter places.

Caucasian from Scandinavia

People in America

The first people to live in America were the ancestors of the American Indians. Around 35,000 years ago, they walked from Asia across the Bering Strait, which was then land, forming a bridge between Asia and America. Gradually, people spread out from the north into South America. American Indians are descended from Asian people, so they have Mongolian features.

North American Indian

South American Indian

People in Australasia

No one lived in Australia until around 38,000 years ago, when Caucasian people arrived there. They either sailed in canoes or walked from Malaysia, which may then have been a bridge of land between Asia and Australia. These people were the ancestors of the Australian Aborigines. In New Zealand, the Maoris descended from Polynesians, who arrived 1,200 years ago.

Aborigine

Maori

Merging cultures

People around the world are different from one another partly because of their looks, but also because of their religion, language, food, music and customs. All of these things put together make up a people's **culture**.

People have always travelled in search of new places in which to settle. Today, many countries have different groups of people living in them. Cultures merge as new people bring customs with them from their old country, but also adopt the culture of their new country.

You can try food from different cultures in the restaurants of most cities.

Endangered peoples

When people settle in new areas, they may disrupt the native way of life. Natives may lose the land off which they live, and then have to adopt the new people's culture. The Inuit, the North and South American Indians and the Aborigines have all suffered in this way. Many of those who have lost their homelands now live in smaller, protected areas called **reservations**.

Rich world, poor world

Over many years, a country gradually develops as its industry improves and its people raise their standard of living.

The countries of the world are at different stages of **development** and there is a great difference between the most and the least developed. Poorer countries are known as **less developed countries** and richer countries are known as **more developed countries**.

In recent years, some countries which were less developed countries have set up modern industries and have become richer. These countries are called **newly industrialized countries**.

This map shows how much of the world is poor. On the map, the areas of the continents are accurate in relation to each other.

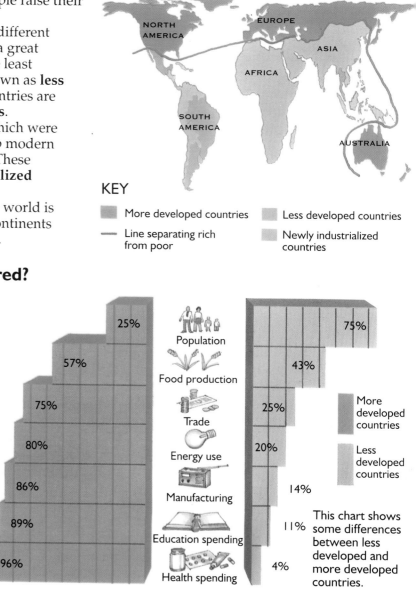

KEY

■ More developed countries
— Line separating rich from poor
■ Less developed countries
■ Newly industrialized countries

How is development measured?

People's daily lives are affected by how much money their country has to spend. So, looking at facts about a country and its people shows how developed it has become.

The bar chart on the right compares some facts about more developed countries and less developed countries. It shows that, although less developed countries have a greater share of the world's population, they produce less food, do less trade, use less energy, and manufacture fewer goods. They also spend far less on schools and hospitals.

Population: 25% / 75%
Food production: 57% / 43%
Trade: 75% / 25%
Energy use: 80% / 20%
Manufacturing: 86% / 14%
Education spending: 89% / 11%
Health spending: 96% / 4%

More developed countries

Less developed countries

This chart shows some differences between less developed and more developed countries.

Life in a poor country

Life in poor countries is often hard. Children spend less time at school and so people are less able to read and write. They may spend much time looking for basic items, such as fuel and water. Water may be polluted and there may not be enough food, which causes malnutrition. There may be few hospitals and high death rates.

The flow chart on the right shows how people in poor countries may easily become trapped in a cycle of poverty and disease.

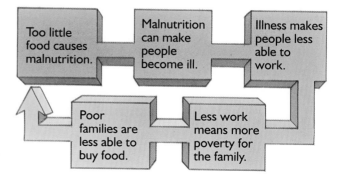

Too little food causes malnutrition.

Malnutrition can make people become ill.

Illness makes people less able to work.

Poor families are less able to buy food.

Less work means more poverty for the family.

56

Why are some countries poor?

Countries are poor for different reasons. Some have few resources such as minerals and crops. In others, there may be mountains, deserts or jungles, or the area may be affected by pests such as locusts, and hazards such as floods. Elsewhere, the climate may be too cold, too hot or too dry. All these things make farming, industry and transport difficult and slow development down.

There are other reasons to do with politics and trade why some countries are poor. Until the mid 1900s, European countries governed over regions, called colonies, around the world. The colonies were used to make Europe rich by providing minerals for industry and food for Europe's growing population. However, the colonies gained little profit. Even today, many industries in poor countries are owned by people from rich countries, who take the profits away from the industry.

This picture shows an example of trade between rich and poorer nations and how the rich ones may make a bigger profit.

Europe

Brazil

Aluminium ingots

1. Brazil, a poorer country, exports aluminium to Europe, Japan and the USA. Some profits go to non-Brazilians, who own shares in the industry.

2. In Europe, aluminium is manufactured into goods, such as saucepans and washing machines.

3. The goods are now worth more than aluminium, because it cost money to make them.

4. Europe sells aluminium goods to Brazil at a higher price than the aluminium, making a bigger profit.

Aid from the rich

Rich countries give aid to help poor countries develop. Aid comes from governments, banks and aid agencies. They give or loan money for big projects, such as building a new dam.

Food and supplies are given to people after disasters, such as floods. This is called **short-term aid** because it helps people who are in immediate need.

Technology is provided by foreign engineers and teachers who work with local people. This is **long-term aid** because people benefit in the future.

Not all aid is good. People may give the wrong aid, such as machines with no spare parts. Or, aid may not be shared out and may not reach those who need it. Some governments lend aid rather than give it, and then only if poor nations promise to buy goods from them.

DID YOU KNOW?

Millions of people around the world become poor because they have to leave their homes and live in a strange city or even another country. These people are called **refugees**. Some become refugees because they cannot find work and others lose their homes in disasters or wars. Many people become refugees because they disagree with their government and are forced to leave their country and seek a new life elsewhere.

Population

A population is the number of people who live in a particular place. The population of the world is about 5 billion (5,000 million). By the year 2025, it will have risen to around 8.5 billion. This means that the world will have to support the needs of over one and a half times as many people as there are today.

The speed at which a population grows is called the **growth rate**. In the past, the world's population grew steadily but slowly. People have estimated that in the 17th century the world's population was about 500 million. Since then, the growth rate has gone up rapidly. The graph shows how the population is changing and how the change will continue.

Population study

Many countries carry out a census once every ten years or so, when everyone fills in a questionnaire about themselves. This helps the government find out how many people live in the country and what their needs will be in the future. People who study population are called **demographers**.

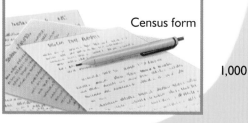

Census form

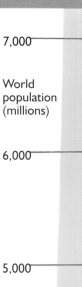

World population (millions)

7,000

6,000

5,000

4,000

3,000

2,000

1,000

Date (year)

| 1200 | 1300 | 1400 | 1500 | 1600 | 1700 | 1800 | 1900 | 2000 |

Population change

The population changes depending on how many people are born and how many die each year. In Australia, around 15 people are born and 7 people die for every thousand people in the population, so its population is growing. These are called the **birth** and **death rates**.

A country's birth and death rates are affected by its standard of health care. If doctors and drugs are available, more babies survive and adults live longer.

Good health care increases the population.

Family planning also affects the population of a country because it allows couples to choose when to have children and also how many children to have.

Family planning controls the population.

Population can be drastically affected if there is a war or a natural disaster. Many people may die during war, famine, an earthquake, a volcanic eruption or a flood.

Wars and natural disasters reduce the population.

People leaving a country are called **emigrants**. Those settling in a new country are called **immigrants**. Population changes according to how many immigrants and emigrants there are.

Immigration and emigration changes the population.

The growing world

The populations of different countries change at different rates. In more developed countries*, such as Japan or the USA, the growth rate is very low. Families are not very large and people live longer because they have good health care.

However, in less developed countries*, the population is growing much faster. It is in these countries that over 90% of the world's population growth is happening. In some of these countries, there is not enough money and food to care for millions of extra people.

In the past, people in poorer countries needed large families to help earn a living, and as some children were expected to die, couples did not want to limit the number of babies they had.

In recent years, health care has improved in these countries, so more people are living longer and more babies are surviving. However, many people are still having large families, so the population is rising fast. These days, couples are encouraged to have fewer children so the population growth will slow down.

This map shows how the population is changing in different areas around the world.

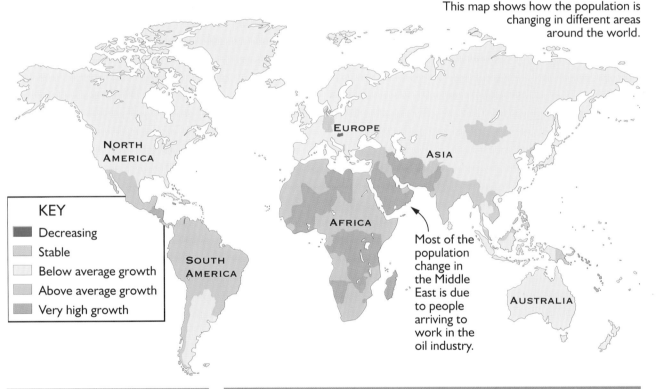

KEY
- Decreasing
- Stable
- Below average growth
- Above average growth
- Very high growth

NORTH AMERICA

EUROPE

ASIA

AFRICA

SOUTH AMERICA

AUSTRALIA

Most of the population change in the Middle East is due to people arriving to work in the oil industry.

DID YOU KNOW?

Each year, the world population grows by over 90 million. This means that it increases by almost three people every second. In the time that it takes you to read this paragraph, there will be enough extra people in the world to make at least two soccer teams.

One-child families

There are 1.2 billion people in China, which is more than in any other country. To help control the population growth, the government introduced a law to make couples have no more than one child. If this law succeeds, brothers, sisters, uncles, aunts and cousins may become rare in China in the future. This Chinese government poster reminds people that they should have only one child.

*Less developed and more developed countries, 56.

Where we live

There are many reasons why people live where they do today and why people settled in those places originally. When people first looked for permanent places to settle long ago, they had to think about what they needed, such as food, water, warmth and shelter. They also had to be able to defend themselves. These maps show how settlers may have chosen a place to build their homes.

The lake supplies fish for food.

Hills make it difficult for enemies to attack a settlement.

This would have been the best site for a settlement.

The river supplies fresh water to drink.

Forest supplies wood for building materials and fuel, and animals to hunt.

Crops can grow and animals can graze on flat, fertile land.

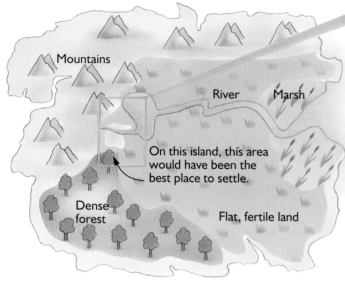

Mountains

River   Marsh

On this island, this area would have been the best place to settle.

Dense forest

Flat, fertile land

First, settlers had to look around to make sure that the area could provide food, water and materials for building and clothes. Early settlements were usually near rivers or springs, and on land where people could raise animals and grow crops.

After deciding on a good area, people had to choose the exact site for their settlement very carefully. They preferred to live in places that were easy to defend, such as hillsides. They also chose places that were protected from floods or bad weather.

Temporary settlements

The first settlements were probably just campsites. People chose a spot near food and water and then built temporary shelters out of materials found close by, such as leaves, branches and animal skins. When food ran out, they moved on to a new spot, leaving their shelters behind. Some groups of people, such as the Maasai of East Africa, still live in temporary settlements.

In the dry season, the Maasai move their cattle on to new grazing land, leaving villages empty.

The Maasai and their cattle come back to their villages in the rainy season.

Hamlets to megacities

Today, people live in all kinds of areas and in settlements of different sizes. They also travel around a lot more. This is because they can obtain food, water and materials wherever they live, due to modern technology. Where people live now depends on where they work, how they travel there and what services* they need nearby.

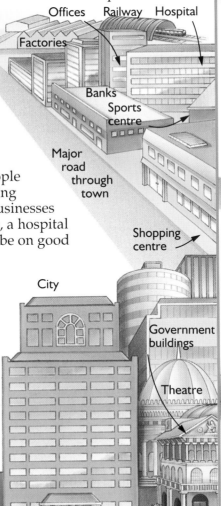

Village

School

Shops

Main Road

Church

Hamlet

Minor road

Farms

Houses

Hamlets are the smallest kind of settlement. They may be just a collection of buildings, perhaps centred around a few farms. There may not even be a shop there.

Offices   Railway   Hospital

Factories

Banks

Sports centre

Major road through town

Shopping centre

City

Government buildings

Theatre

University

Business headquarters

Villages may centre around farms, with several hundred people living there. They may have a few shops and a place of worship. Large villages may have a school.

Towns may have thousands of people living in them. They have a shopping centre or market, and also many businesses and special services, such as banks, a hospital and a sports centre. They will also be on good transport routes.

Cities are the centre of local government, business, culture* and religion. Each city has different zones (areas), such as residential areas with houses, industrial areas with factories and commercial areas with shops and banks. Cities with populations of over a million are called **megacities**. Mexico City is the largest, with nearly 20 million people.

Traditional homes

Wherever people settled in the world, they had to use local materials to build shelters. They had to design their homes to suit their environment and climate. Here are some examples of traditional homes which developed in certain areas.

Igloo

The Inuit, who live in the Arctic, needed shelter from the cold, but had few materials to build with. So they built igloos from blocks of ice.

Log cabin

In northern Europe, people were surrounded by plenty of wood, so they built log cabins. The roofs were steep so that heavy snow would slide off in winter.

Tent

In hot desert regions, people had to move around to find water and food. Nomads* made tents to shelter under, which could be packed away and moved.

*Culture, 55; nomads, 43; services, 78.

Villages and towns

Just over half of the world's population lives in villages in **rural** areas (the countryside). Most of these people live in less developed countries* in Africa and Asia and earn their living by farming. However, many people are leaving the traditional villages and going to work in **urban** areas (towns). This map shows where most people live in rural areas and where most people live in urban areas. Areas with a mostly urban population are not always crowded with people. The towns in those areas may be quite spread out.

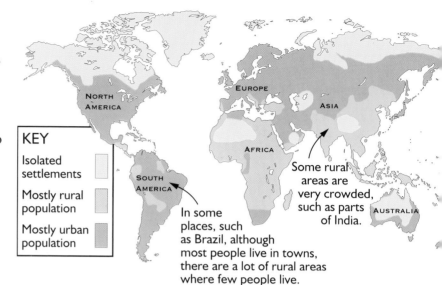

KEY

Isolated settlements

Mostly rural population

Mostly urban population

Some rural areas are very crowded, such as parts of India.

In some places, such as Brazil, although most people live in towns, there are a lot of rural areas where few people live.

How towns grow

Originally, people built their homes close together in villages for companionship and safety. Living close together meant that they could also share services*. Over a long period of time, many villages grow into towns. There is usually a good reason why this growth happens. This picture shows some examples.

Coastal villages may grow if there are good fishing grounds off the coast or if there is a good harbour.

Villages near bridges or fords grow as travellers pass through to use the crossing.

Many people travel through crossroads. This causes shops and services to grow there.

Villages that are in between several other villages grow because they are good meeting points and market-places.

Village patterns

In different parts of the world, village houses and other buildings are clustered together in different patterns.

In parts of Africa, houses are arranged around a circular space called a kraal. Cattle are kept inside the kraal at night.

Kraal

Village on high strip of land

Closely-packed village

In lowland areas, like some parts of Europe, houses may be built on the higher strips of land, which are safe from floods. The low-lying land is then used for farming.

In places that have little good farmland available, like Japan, village buildings may be packed closely together. This saves more space for farming.

*Less developed countries, 56; services, 78.

Town planning

Old towns may become too cramped for modern traffic and for the amount of people who live and work in them. To keep towns up-to-date, people called **town planners** decide what changes need to be made.

Every town has its own needs, which town planners have to consider. For example, a holiday resort needs hotels where people can stay. A university town needs cheap housing for students to rent.

Towns may be surrounded by an area of countryside, called a **green belt**. Planners make sure that the town does not expand into the green belt. They also make sure that valuable, old buildings are preserved.

If there is no room for a town to expand, and space is needed for new industries and homes, governments may build brand-new towns. These are called **satellite towns** because they are built in the surroundings of old cities.

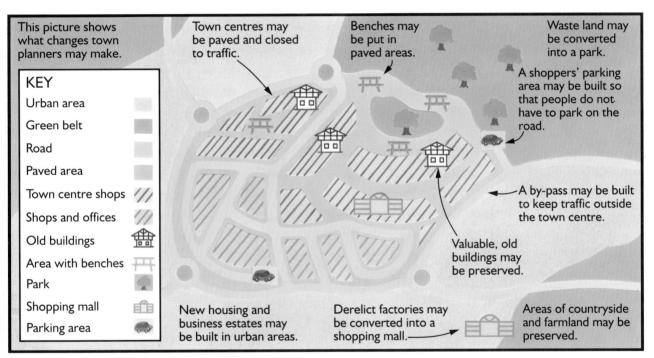

This picture shows what changes town planners may make.

Town centres may be paved and closed to traffic.

Benches may be put in paved areas.

Waste land may be converted into a park.

A shoppers' parking area may be built so that people do not have to park on the road.

A by-pass may be built to keep traffic outside the town centre.

Valuable, old buildings may be preserved.

New housing and business estates may be built in urban areas.

Derelict factories may be converted into a shopping mall.

Areas of countryside and farmland may be preserved.

KEY

Urban area
Green belt
Road
Paved area
Town centre shops
Shops and offices
Old buildings
Area with benches
Park
Shopping mall
Parking area

Boom towns and ghost towns

If a town becomes rich fast, it is called a **boom town**. Many new people and industries may arrive suddenly. If an area becomes poor, towns which were busy can become deserted. These are called **ghost towns**.

For example, when gold was discovered in the USA in 1848, towns grew up all over California. When the mines ran out of gold, trade stopped. Many of the once prosperous towns were abandoned.

Boom town

Ghost town

DID YOU KNOW?

Some towns do not have a good geographical reason for growing. Clermont-Ferrand in France became a wealthy tyre-producing town, even though it is a long way from other manufacturing areas and it is inland, away from its sources of raw materials*. However, Mr Michelin, who founded the tyre-producing business, chose Clermont-Ferrand because he happened to live there.

*Raw materials, 76.

63

Cities

In Greek and Roman times, the population of a city was only a few thousand. Cities did not become much bigger until the Industrial Revolution in the 1800s, when transport and industry suddenly expanded. Now, many cities have over a million people living in them.

A city develops when it becomes a focus for its region and outgrows other towns. Many cities grow on major transport routes, where people meet to trade. The city then becomes a centre of business and government. Chicago, in the USA, grew in the mid 1800s because it became the centre of transport, services* and industry between the new farms on the prairies and the old eastern cities, such as Boston, New York and Washington.

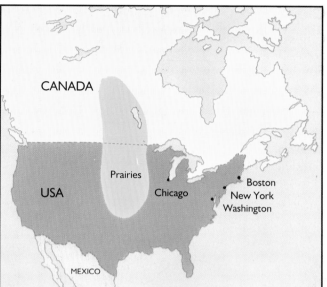

In the 1880s, ten years after diamonds were discovered, Kimberley was already a small town.

Diamond mines →

Kimberley

Railway

Miles　0.5

Km　0.5　1

Other cities grow because they are educational or religious centres, or because they have important resources and industry there. These things bring people into an area to work or to visit. In South Africa, the town of Kimberley was built after diamonds were discovered there. There was no settlement at all beforehand, but the diamond industry has made it a busy city.

Transport improvements help cities spread out. If a new transport route is built, more people can live outside the city centre and travel in to work. New residential areas, called **suburbs**, are then built around the city. London, in the UK, spread out along transport routes in the early 1900s.

London in the 1930s

London in the 1890s

River Thames

Capital cities

Every nation has a capital city, which is an important city for that country. It is the place of government and may also be the focus of the country's culture*.

Some countries have replaced their old capitals by building new, modern cities. They are designed to be practical and spacious. Canberra in Australia, Islamabad in Pakistan and Brasilia in Brazil are all new capitals.

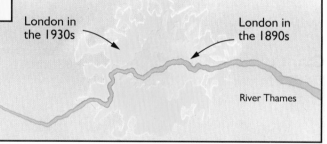

Brasilia is built in the shape of a plane.

Wide roads are built to cope with busy traffic.

Government buildings are all together so that officials can communicate easily.

Lake Paranoà

City zones

Cities can be divided into different areas or zones. Each zone has its own particular purpose. For example, it may be mostly residential, with houses, or it may be mostly industrial, with factories. Here are some main areas which you can see in most cities.

The middle of the city is where most shops, banks and offices are. This area is called the **central business district (CBD)**. Most of the trade and financial business goes on there. People travel into the CBD to work.

Around the CBD, there may be industrial zones of older industries. Circled around these may be residential areas. The older areas near the middle may decay and become redeveloped into houses, shops or offices.

The newer suburbs are on the city edge.

Areas of light industry*, shops and other businesses may line the major roads leading out of the city.

The city may grow so large that areas on the edge become centres too, with their own zone patterns.

Giant cities

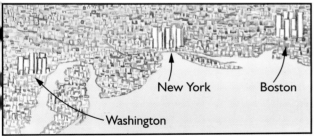

New York

Boston

Washington

As cities grow, they spread out into the countryside. Eventually, towns and cities may merge and become one huge urban area, called a **conurbation**. The biggest urban area in the world is in the USA. The towns almost join for 625km (390 miles) from Boston, through New York, to Washington. Some people call this area Bosnywash, from the first letters in each name.

Poverty in the city

All around the world, people move to cities to find work. However, they may have nowhere to live when they arrive. Some of these newcomers build makeshift homes. In less developed countries*, many cities are surrounded by areas of makeshift homes called **shanty towns**. These are very crowded and may have no clean water or power supply.

In shanty towns, people make homes from whatever they can find, such as scrap metal and cardboard.

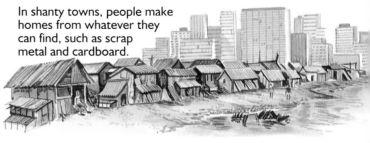

Less developed countries, 56; light industry, 76.

65

Farming around the world

Most of the food we eat, and some of the things we use, come from farms. Different types of goods come from different places around the world, because each area has its own particular environment where certain plants and animals like to live.

Farmers need to grow crops and raise animals that are suited to their land. They need to think about what the climate is like, what type of soil there is and how hilly the land is. In the picture are some of the questions they need to ask themselves.

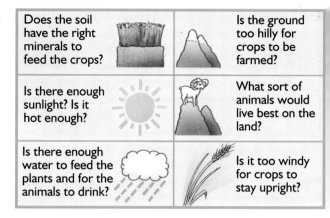

Does the soil have the right minerals to feed the crops?

Is the ground too hilly for crops to be farmed?

Is there enough sunlight? Is it hot enough?

What sort of animals would live best on the land?

Is there enough water to feed the plants and for the animals to drink?

Is it too windy for crops to stay upright?

Types of farm

People who only grow crops are **arable farmers**. Those who only keep animals are **livestock farmers**. Some do both and are called **mixed farmers**. The size of farms around the world varies too. The map shows what type of farm is most common in each area of the world.

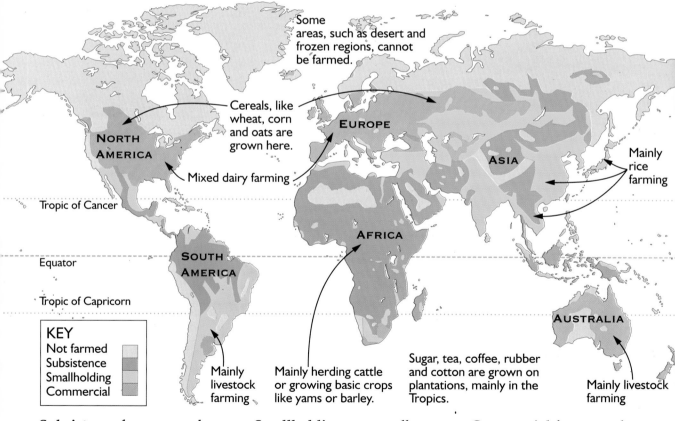

Some areas, such as desert and frozen regions, cannot be farmed.

Cereals, like wheat, corn and oats are grown here.

EUROPE

NORTH AMERICA

Mixed dairy farming

Tropic of Cancer

ASIA

Mainly rice farming

AFRICA

Equator

SOUTH AMERICA

Tropic of Capricorn

AUSTRALIA

KEY
Not farmed
Subsistence
Smallholding
Commercial

Mainly livestock farming

Mainly herding cattle or growing basic crops like yams or barley.

Sugar, tea, coffee, rubber and cotton are grown on plantations, mainly in the Tropics.

Mainly livestock farming

Subsistence farmers produce enough to feed their families but have nothing left to sell. Some subsistence farmers move from place to place. This is called **shifting cultivation**.

Smallholdings are small areas of land farmed by a family or a small company. They sell food to local people or to bigger firms which transport goods to shops further away.

Commercial farms produce very large amounts of food to sell to supermarkets and food manufacturers. **Plantations** are huge commercial farms that grow just one crop.

Going shopping

If you go into a supermarket, you will find many different kinds of goods that have come from all over the world. Countries buy food from each other so that people have a bigger choice of things to eat and drink.

North America produces flour from its wheat fields.

Some food is from a variety of countries, like the fruit in cans of mixed fruit.

Bananas may grow on smallholdings in hot places like the West Indies.

Tea is grown on plantations in hot places like India and Sri Lanka.

Lamb comes from places with mild weather and good grass, like England or New Zealand.

FLOUR

The Netherlands has many dairy farms which make cheese.

Oranges and lemons are grown in warm places, like Spain and Portugal.

Coffee grows on plantations in hot places, like Brazil and Kenya.

Farming in the past

The first humans hunted wild animals and gathered the stems, leaves and berries of wild plants.

Early plough

People learned how to tame animals and plant crops. They invented machinery to help them, like the plough. Ploughs turn soil over and leave a furrow so that seeds can be put in the ground.

To keep food fresh, refrigerated trucks may be used to transport it.

Communities traded with each other by taking food to local markets. Today, people transport food across great distances.

A banana's journey

...washed and packed...

...where they are sold.

Bananas are picked...

...and shipped abroad...

Many bananas are grown in the West Indies. When it is time for the bananas to be cut down, almost everyone from the local village helps, even the children.

They take the bananas to a local boxing plant, where they are washed and packed. Big firms buy the best bananas to sell abroad at a profit.

The bananas are transported inside huge refrigerators on ships and trucks. This keeps them fresh on their long journey to the shops.

More about farming

Farmers try to produce as much as they can from their land. To do this, they adapt and improve the natural environment so that they get a bigger harvest. They may even be able to produce crops which would not normally grow well in their particular region.

In cooler countries, farmers can bring extra heat to their plants by keeping them in a glass or plastic greenhouse. Greenhouses trap warmth so it is possible to grow things in them that would normally need a warmer season or climate to survive.

Fruit and salad vegetables may be grown in greenhouses.

Fertilizer spreader

Manure spreader

Tractors pull machinery over the fields.

Chemical sprayer

Farmers can add nutrients, called **fertilizers**, to the soil to help it stay fertile. Animal manure and compost (rotting plants) are good substances for this purpose. Fertilizers can also be made artificially from chemicals.

Many farmers spray crops with chemicals called **pesticides** to control weeds, disease and insects. The crops grow better but it is possible that traces of pesticides are left in food.

Many people worry in case artificial chemicals harm their health. **Organic farms** produce food without using artificial chemicals in crop sprays or animal feed.

Caring for the soil

Fertile soil is rich in nutrients. Different plants, like wheat and sugar-beet, use up different kinds of nutrients. So, to keep the soil fertile, farmers change the crops grown in each field every year. This is called **crop rotation**. Some crops, like clover, are good at putting nutrients back into the soil. This plan shows how crop rotation works.

KEY			Field A	Field B	Field C
Wheat		Year 1	Wheat	Sugar-beet	Clover
Sugar-beet		Year 2	Clover	Wheat	Sugar-beet
Clover		Year 3	Sugar-beet	Clover	Wheat

Watering the plants

Plants need water to grow. When there is not enough water in the soil, farmers bring it to the crops by artificial means. This is called **irrigation**.

The Ancient Egyptians were the first to use irrigation. They invented ways to transport water from the River Nile to the fields. Some of their methods, such as the Archimedean Screw, are still in use today.

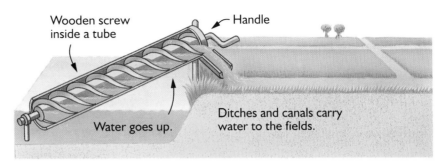

Wooden screw inside a tube

Handle

Water goes up.

Ditches and canals carry water to the fields.

The Archimedean Screw is a big, wooden screw inside a tube, which has one end lying in a river. Someone turns the

handle of the screw. This forces water up the tube, through a pipe and into a ditch leading to the fields.

Extensive farming

In places like Australia and North America where there is lots of inexpensive land, farmers run big farms which produce huge amounts of food. These farms need few workers because big machines do much of the work and the farmers grow crops and raise animals which do not need close care. This is called **extensive farming**.

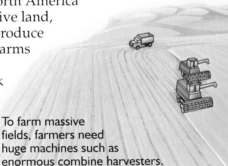

To farm massive fields, farmers need huge machines such as enormous combine harvesters.

Intensive farming

Intensively reared chickens are kept in cages, where food is brought to them.

In places like Europe, where there is less land available, farms may be smaller. Huge machines are not suitable on small farms. Instead, farmers may use more workers and grow more crops or animals per unit of land. They farm the land all year and produce goods that sell at high prices. This is called **intensive farming**.

Steps in the land

Terraces are steps cut in a hillside. They make work easier on hilly land and make more land usable. Terracing is used, for example, in the rice fields of South East Asia.

Farming technology

Scientists have found a way to grow plants by choosing which features they will inherit. This process, called **genetic engineering**, helps them grow lots of high quality plants.

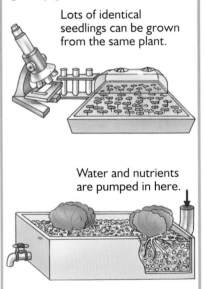

Lots of identical seedlings can be grown from the same plant.

Water and nutrients are pumped in here.

Plants can be grown in polythene or gravel instead of soil. Nutrients and water are pumped past their roots, so they grow well. This is called **hydroponics**.

Forestry and fishing

People have always used wood and fished the oceans. Today, forestry and fishing are huge industries which employ lots of people and provide many useful things.

Centuries ago, much of the land was covered in forest. Over the years, people have cut trees down for fuel, building materials and to make room for farming. Forests have become smaller and some have even disappeared altogether.

Many forests are still being destroyed because they are not managed properly. To look after forests, people must limit how many trees are felled and also plant new trees to replace them.

This picture shows the cycle of how forests are managed.

Young trees grow into mature trees.

Young trees are planted.

Mature trees are chopped down.

Why we need trees

Trees are not just needed for wood. They do many important things, such as releasing oxygen for living things to breathe.

Many birds and other wild animals make their homes in trees.

Trees stop wind from blowing dry soil away.

Leaves give out oxygen.

Trees are a barrier against heavy rain damaging the soil.

Roots soak up water so that top-soil is not washed away.

Trees protect soil from wind and rain. Roots help to bind soil together. Also, rubber, some waxes, resins, gums and many medicines come from trees.

The world's forests

Different forests grow in different climates. In cool areas, forests of conifers grow, called **boreal forests**. **Temperate forest** grows in mild regions and can be made of conifers, deciduous trees or a mixture of both. Rainforest* (tropical and equatorial forest) grows in hot, rainy places. Thousands of different types of trees grow in rainforests.

Conifers have needle-like leaves.

Deciduous trees have broad, flat leaves.

Rainforest has many types of trees.

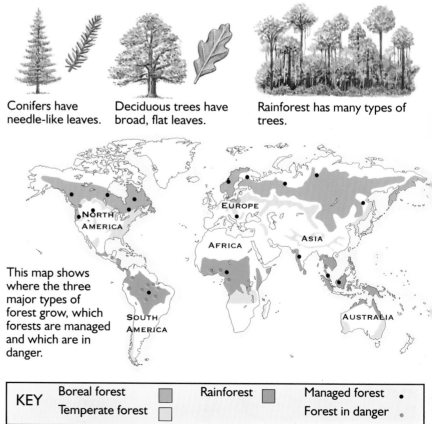

NORTH AMERICA

EUROPE

ASIA

AFRICA

SOUTH AMERICA

AUSTRALIA

This map shows where the three major types of forest grow, which forests are managed and which are in danger.

KEY	Boreal forest		Rainforest		Managed forest	•
	Temperate forest				Forest in danger	•

*Rainforest, 42.

Fishing

Every year, about 70 million tonnes (tons) of fish and other sea animals are caught from the oceans. The biggest fishing fleets in the world are owned by Japan and Russia. Below are the main types of sea animals that are caught.

Fish that live near the surface, like this tuna, are called **pelagic fish**. About 30 million tonnes (tons) are caught every year.

Sea animals that have many tentacles (arms), like this octopus, are called **cephalopods**. About one million tonnes (tons) are caught each year.

Sea animals that have hard shells, like this lobster, are called **crustaceans**. About 2.5 million tonnes (tons) are caught each year.

Fish that live near the bottom of the sea, like this cod, are called **demersal** fish. About 20 million tonnes (tons) are caught each year.

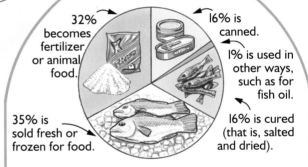

How we use fish

32% becomes fertilizer or animal food.

16% is canned.

1% is used in other ways, such as for fish oil.

16% is cured (that is, salted and dried).

35% is sold fresh or frozen for food.

Fishing efficiency

Large fishing fleets may have a factory ship which cleans and freezes the fish. This means the fleet can stay out at sea longer and catch more. Modern ships use echo-sounding to trace fish shoals (groups). A beam of sound is sent down into the water and then echoes back off the fish. A computer detects where the echo comes from.

Factory ship

A screen image shows where the fish are.

Fish for the future

If fishermen catch too many fish, there will not be enough left in the seas for the future. This is called overfishing. To avoid it, they use nets with large holes so that young fish can escape and breed.

Instead of taking fish from the sea, people can also breed them in fish farms. This is cheaper and safer than sea-fishing and it means that stocks of fish can be controlled and not run down too low. Fish such as salmon, trout and lobster can be bred in coastal waters, rivers and lakes.

71

Mining the Earth

Mining the Earth's crust* produces the rocks and minerals* that industries use for making goods. They are some of our most valuable raw materials*. There are many kinds of rocks and minerals beneath the Earth's surface, which are useful in a variety of ways.

Some rocks and minerals provide energy. Coal, oil and natural gas are fossil fuels*. Uranium is a nuclear fuel.

Gemstones are found inside rocks. Many are rare and valuable. They are cut and polished before use.

Uranium ore

Gold may be found in a pure state.

Corundum rock which contains ruby

Cut diamond

Cut ruby

Iron is found as an ore.

Limestone

Sandstone

Chalk

Many rocks are mined for building. Some, such as sandstone, are cut up and used as they are. Others are mixed to make new building materials, such as limestone and chalk, which are used in cement.

Metals are often found as **ores**, mixed with other rock materials, rather than in a pure state. Metal is separated from ore by heating in a furnace. This is called **smelting**.

Types of mining

In the 1800s, miners dug shallow, sloping tunnels into the hillside to reach rocks and minerals, such as gold. They are called **drift**, or **adit**, **mines**. Some are still used today.

Minerals that are just beneath the surface, such as copper, are mined by digging huge, wide holes in the ground. These are called **open-cast mines**, or **quarries**.

Some materials, such as coal, are found deep underground. To reach them, miners dig **shaft mines**. From these shafts, tunnels stretch for great distances.

Many reservoirs of oil and gas are trapped between rocks under the seabed. To mine oil and gas, which are important energy resources, engineers build rigs in the sea to drill the seabed. Pipes carry the oil and gas to refineries on land where they are processed.

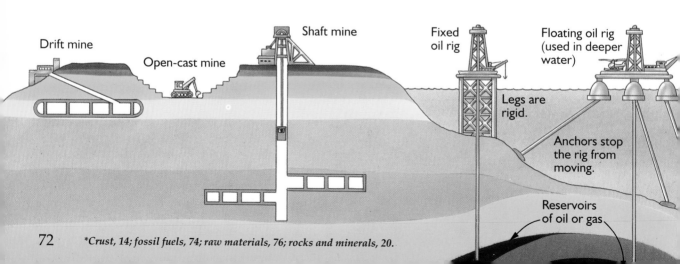

Drift mine

Open-cast mine

Shaft mine

Fixed oil rig

Floating oil rig (used in deeper water)

Legs are rigid.

Anchors stop the rig from moving.

Reservoirs of oil or gas

*Crust, 14; fossil fuels, 74; raw materials, 76; rocks and minerals, 20.

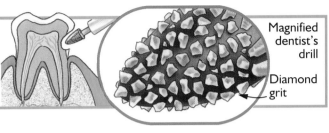

DID YOU KNOW?

Diamonds are very hard stones. Some are used as a cutting edge on tools. For example, a dentist's drill is covered with diamond grit.

Magnified dentist's drill

Diamond grit

Where things are mined

Different areas of the world are rich in different types of rocks and minerals. The map below shows which places produce the largest amounts of some well-known materials.

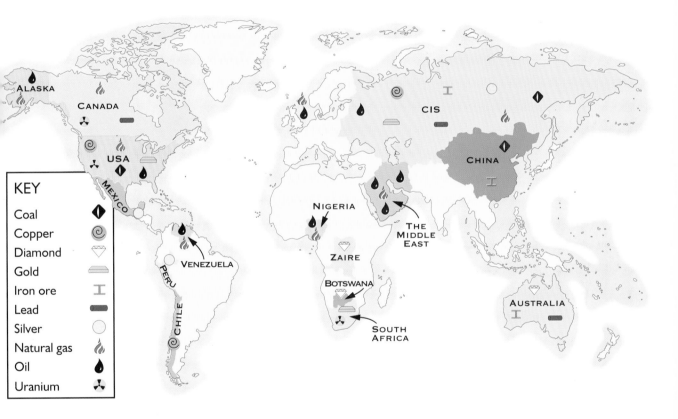

KEY

Coal	◈
Copper	◉
Diamond	⬦
Gold	▭
Iron ore	I
Lead	▬
Silver	○
Natural gas	🔥
Oil	⬤
Uranium	☢

Raw materials running low

This picture shows in which year geologists think our present materials may run out, if they continue to be used at today's rate.

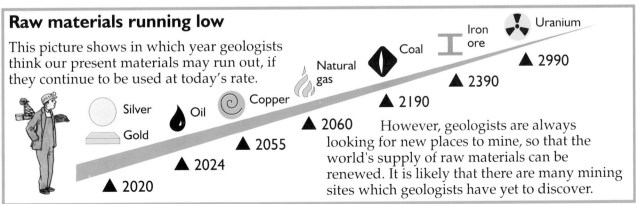

Silver

Gold

Oil

Copper

Natural gas

Coal

Iron ore

Uranium

▲ 2020

▲ 2024

▲ 2055

▲ 2060

▲ 2190

▲ 2390

▲ 2990

However, geologists are always looking for new places to mine, so that the world's supply of raw materials can be renewed. It is likely that there are many mining sites which geologists have yet to discover.

73

Energy

Most of the world's energy comes from coal, oil and natural gas, which are called **fossil fuels**. This type of energy is called **non-renewable energy** because once used, it cannot be reused. For example, once a piece of coal has been burned, it can no longer produce any energy. Fossil fuels cause pollution*, but people still use them because world energy needs are so great.

Unlike fossil fuels, **renewable energy**, such as wind, water, the Sun and heat from inside the Earth, can be reused. For example, water can be used over again to drive a water wheel. The pie chart below shows the percentages of different types of energy used by homes and industry.

Renewable energy 5%

Nuclear energy 3%

Wood 15%

Fossil fuels 77%

Energy from wood 15%

Trees use energy from the Sun to grow. When wood is burned, energy is released as heat. In many poor areas, such as Ethiopia and Nepal, nearly 90% of energy comes from wood.

Fossil fuels 77%

Coal, oil and natural gas are non-renewable fossil fuels. They were formed over millions of years from fossilized* animals and plants. Like wood, fossil fuels release heat energy when burned. Both fossil fuels and wood release gases which can harm the atmosphere.

Nuclear energy 3%

Nuclear energy is produced when atoms (tiny particles) of a nuclear fuel, such as uranium, are split apart. This releases huge amounts of heat from tiny amounts of fuel. However, nuclear energy can be dangerous because the fuel gives off radioactive particles which damage living things.

Renewable energy – see next page 5%

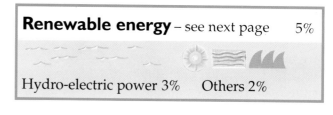

Hydro-electric power 3%   Others 2%

Power stations

Most electricity is produced in power stations. Both fossil fuel and nuclear power stations use fuels to make heat. The picture shows how this heat makes electricity.

Power stations are usually built close to their fuel source, or near good transport links, such as a main railway line or a port. They use a great deal of water for cooling, so they also need to be near large rivers or the sea.

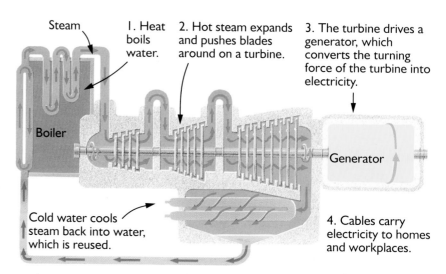

Steam

1. Heat boils water.

2. Hot steam expands and pushes blades around on a turbine.

3. The turbine drives a generator, which converts the turning force of the turbine into electricity.

Boiler

Generator

Cold water cools steam back into water, which is reused.

4. Cables carry electricity to homes and workplaces.

Renewable energy

Renewable energy makes less pollution than non-renewable energy, but at the moment not enough is turned into power to meet all the world's needs. This kind of energy is also called alternative energy because, although it is not greatly used now, it may be a good source of energy for the future. The main forms of renewable energy are shown below.

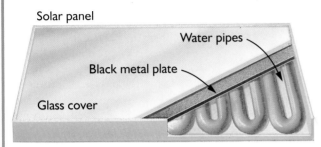

Solar panel

Water pipes

Black metal plate

Glass cover

Solar energy

Solar panels are built on some buildings to absorb and use the Sun's heat. The heat warms black metal plates, which then heat the water pipes behind. Glass covers keep the heat in.

Solar cells power some machines, such as calculators and satellites, by turning the Sun's energy directly into electricity.

Hydro-electric power

In mountain areas of places such as Canada, where there are fast streams, dams can be built to control the water flow. When the water is released, it can generate electricity by turning the blades on a turbine, as shown on the right. This is called **hydro-electric power**, or **HEP**.

HEP stations have a dam which creates a reservoir of water.

Water pours down from the reservoir and drives the turbines.

Energy from underground

Heat from hot rocks in the Earth's crust* can generate electricity, as shown on the right. Cold water is pumped down through boreholes in the rock and steam comes back up, which drives a turbine. This is called **geothermal power**. It is used in places such as New Zealand and Iceland.

Cold water goes down.

Hot rock

Steam comes up.

Wind power

The wind can produce electricity by turning blades on big wind turbines like the one on the right. They work best where wind is very strong. However, it takes thousands of wind turbines to make as much energy as a fossil fuel power station.

Wind turbine

Turbines at sea

The sea can also provide power. The up and down motion of the waves can work machines which drive a turbine. The machine shown on the right is called a nodding duck.

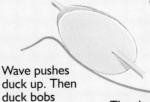

Wave pushes duck up. Then duck bobs down again.

The shaft turns a turbine, which is connected to it.

The in and out motion of the tides can also drive a turbine, as shown on the left. Tidal power is used in the La Rance Estuary in France, where there is a big difference between high and low tide.

Tide going in.

Tide going out.

Manufacturing

Making new products is called **manufacturing**. The materials that are used in making new products are called **raw materials**.

In the past, people manufactured things in their own homes. Then, in the 1700s, a steam engine which could power big machines was developed. The new machinery made products more quickly and cheaply than human-powered machines. Employers built factories for the machines and paid people to work in them.

Home spinning wheel

Machine spinning at the factory

The first factories were in the UK, because the machines were invented there. After the arrival of these machines, fewer people worked at home because they could not make a profit. This time of change is known as the **Industrial Revolution**. These days, most countries manufacture goods in factories. However, some people still manufacture goods at home, especially in parts of the world where human labour is far cheaper than machine power.

Heavy or light?

Manufacturing industries are divided into two types. **Heavy industries**, such as ship-building, use large machines and heavy raw materials.

Light fabrics used in clothes-making

Heavy steel used in ship-building

Industries such as clothes-making which use light raw materials and produce light goods, are called **light industries**.

Choosing a location

When a company builds a new factory, it has to choose the area carefully. Where will the workers, customers and raw materials come from? Is there a power supply and good road and rail links?

Is there an airport or seaport nearby to import and export goods (bring goods in and out of the country)? This map shows where different kinds of factories may be found.

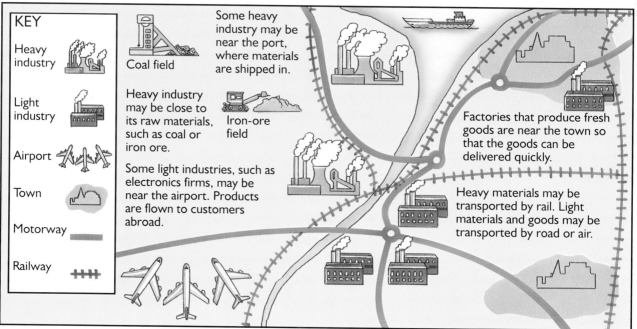

KEY

Heavy industry

Light industry

Airport

Town

Motorway

Railway

Coal field

Some heavy industry may be near the port, where materials are shipped in.

Heavy industry may be close to its raw materials, such as coal or iron ore.

Iron-ore field

Some light industries, such as electronics firms, may be near the airport. Products are flown to customers abroad.

Factories that produce fresh goods are near the town so that the goods can be delivered quickly.

Heavy materials may be transported by rail. Light materials and goods may be transported by road or air.

International companies

A company with factories in different countries is called a **multinational**. Many motor companies are multinationals, with factories in different places making different parts of cars. These are then put together at an assembly plant. The picture shows how parts may come from many places.

Multinationals have some advantages over companies that are based in one country. More workers and customers are available to them and they can sell goods more easily in countries where they own a factory. They can also make each part of their product where it is cheapest to do so.

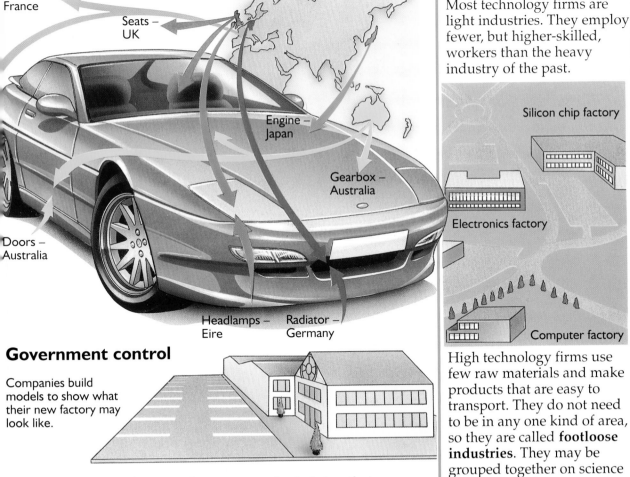

Assembled in the UK

Bumpers – France

Seats – UK

Engine – Japan

Gearbox – Australia

Doors – Australia

Headlamps – Eire

Radiator – Germany

High technology

Manufacturers of products like electronic equipment and computers are called **high technology industries**. They use the latest ideas and skills for their work.

High technology products

Most technology firms are light industries. They employ fewer, but higher-skilled, workers than the heavy industry of the past.

Silicon chip factory

Electronics factory

Computer factory

High technology firms use few raw materials and make products that are easy to transport. They do not need to be in any one kind of area, so they are called **footloose industries**. They may be grouped together on science parks where they can provide materials and services* for each other. Universities may be nearby to help think up new ideas.

Government control

Companies build models to show what their new factory may look like.

Governments sometimes study plans for new factories before they are built. They may encourage new factories in an area which needs more jobs. They may also help foreign companies to bring their business into the country. If a factory will spoil an area by polluting it or by making it look ugly, governments can stop it from being built.

*Services, 78.

77

Services

Anyone who has a job doing or supplying something for other people is providing a **service**. In some countries, plenty of services are available and many people are employed doing them. In other countries, people do most things for themselves.

What services are there?

This picture shows some of the people who supply services around the town and what sort of services are supplied.

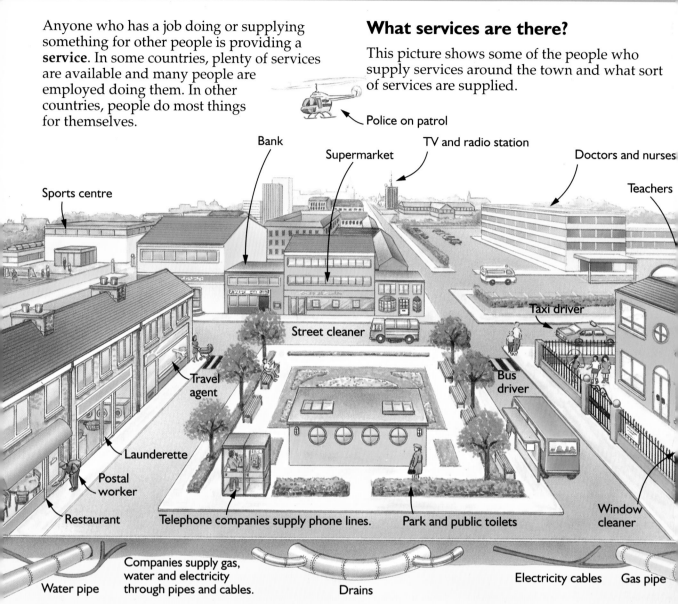

Police on patrol

Sports centre

Bank

Supermarket

TV and radio station

Doctors and nurses

Teachers

Travel agent

Street cleaner

Taxi driver

Bus driver

Launderette

Postal worker

Restaurant

Telephone companies supply phone lines.

Park and public toilets

Window cleaner

Water pipe

Companies supply gas, water and electricity through pipes and cables.

Drains

Electricity cables

Gas pipe

City services

Cities are organized for providing lots of different services. Some services may be grouped together in areas which are known for providing that type of service. For example, a city may have an entertainment district, a retail area with shops, and a financial sector with banks and finance companies.

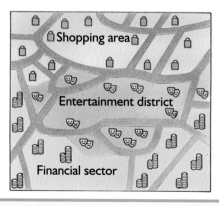

Shopping area

Entertainment district

Financial sector

Out-of-town shopping

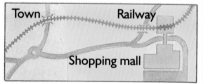

Town

Railway

Shopping mall

If space runs out in a town, people may build out-of-town shopping areas. Many services are together in one place and there is plenty of parking space for cars.

Richer or poorer?

In richer countries, there are usually more workers employed in service jobs than in poorer countries. This is because the people there have more leisure time and can afford to pay for things like hobbies and travel, which create service jobs. This picture shows the percentage of workers who do service jobs in some different countries.

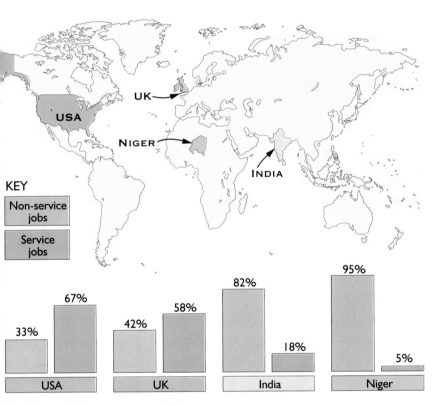

KEY

Non-service jobs

Service jobs

USA 33% / 67%

UK 42% / 58%

India 82% / 18%

Niger 95% / 5%

Doing things yourself

In poorer countries, some villages may have only a few basic services available. People have to do most things for themselves and have no spare time or money.

There may be no electricity, so people use wood for heating and cooking. People get their water for cooking and washing from a well.

A doctor may come only once a year and if there is no local transport, children may walk a long way to get to their school.

In poorer countries, women may spend hours finding fuel, food and water.

Computerized services

Today, many service jobs are done with the help of computers. Computers speed things up and make people's jobs easier. For example, people can withdraw money from a bank's computerized cash machine instead of being served by a bank clerk.

In many stores, scanners at the check-out register the prices of goods by reading computer codes. Assistants no longer have to key in the prices.

Scanner

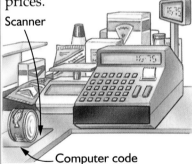

Computer code

Cash registers record how much is sold, so that no one has to count the stock.

Bus and train tickets may be sold and collected by computerized machines instead of by transport workers.

Transport

Centuries ago, much of the land was covered in forest. The easiest way to move around was to travel along the rivers, so canoes were probably the first vehicles to be built. Today they are still the best way to travel through areas of thick jungle.

On land, animals used to provide the only form of transport. In countries where there are few motor vehicles, people still ride on animals and use them to pull carts. For example, oxen are used in places such as India and Thailand.

Oxen can pull heavy loads.

As steam engines developed in the early 1800s, machines began to replace animals as the best form of transport. Roads became better too with the invention of new materials such as tarmac. Transport then improved quickly as people began to want to move goods around and travel more.

Today, many people rely on modern transport. If there were no cars, ships, trains and planes, people would have much less choice in where to live, work and spend their leisure time.

Travelling across sky...

Air travel began with hot air balloons. In the late 1800s, powered airships were invented.

Airship

The first plane flight was made in 1903. Planes then improved quickly when they were needed in World War I (1914-18).

World War I plane

Today, the passenger jet *Concorde* can fly at twice the speed of sound.

Concorde

...sea...

Paddle-steamer

In the late 1700s, paddle-steamers travelled on rivers in France and the USA.

From the 1840s, ocean liners were built. By the 1930s, they were crossing the Atlantic in about four days.

Ocean liner

Today, people seldom travel by ocean liner. For short journeys, they use car ferries or hydrofoils.

Hydrofoil

...and land

The first trains, in the early 1800s, carried goods. They travelled at less than 16kmph (10mph).

The *Rocket* – one of the first trains

The first car was built by Karl Benz in 1885. It could travel no faster than 16kmph (10mph).

Benz's car

Modern cars and trains can travel a long way at high speed. They are comfortable and reliable.

Modern sports car

Passenger travel

Many people travel short distances to nearby places every day. They need cheap and reliable transport, so they use cars, trains, buses or trams which stop locally.

City-centre tram

Fast train

For longer distances, people sometimes need faster transport. Trains, coaches and also planes travel directly between cities, with few stops.

Passenger jet

When people need to travel great distances in a short time, the best way to go is by plane, though it may be expensive. Planes may fly over continents without stopping.

Carrying goods

Planes only carry a certain weight, so heavy goods are transported around the world by ship, truck or train. These take longer to reach their destination, but they are much cheaper to use.

Cargo truck

Owning a car

Motor vehicles give people freedom over where and when they travel. In rich countries, many adults own vehicles. In poor ones, more people walk, use cheap mopeds or local transport. The graph below shows approximately what percentage of people own cars in some different countries.

% of people who own a car

Canada	45%
Greece	14%
Thailand	1.5%
Kenya	0.5%

Traffic jams

In many places, the roads are clogged up with traffic. In some cities, such as Athens and Los Angeles, traffic is causing serious pollution*. This causes damage to health and to the environment. To help solve these problems, people could walk or cycle more often. Governments could also encourage people to use public transport rather than cars.

Exhaust gases eat away at brick and stone.

Routes

A network of roads and other routes connects places around the world. Some routes have been used for hundreds of years and are still in use today. Others have been built especially for today's modern transport.

The quickest way to get from one place to another is to travel along a straight, level route. However, obstacles in the landscape, such as hills, rivers, forests and towns, make it impossible to travel always in a straight line. These two pages show some ways to take routes around obstacles.

It may be possible to dig part of a hill away to make a cutting for a road, canal or railway.

Travelling through a busy town slows traffic down. By going around a ring-road or a by-pass, traffic avoids the town.

People can cut clearings in forests to make room for roads or railways.

Bridges called **viaducts** carry railways across obstacles such as rivers.

Roads and railways

Cities and towns are linked by roads and railways. Roads take people from door to door, while trains only stop at certain places. Railway journeys, though, are fast because the track is as straight and flat as possible.

People may travel up and down high mountains by cable car.

The distance up and down a hill is longer than the distance straight through it. So, going through a tunnel is usually the fastest route to the other side.

Roads may wind up around a hill to make the route less steep.

Roman roads

The Romans were expert road builders. They built roads as straight as possible. Many modern roads run along old Roman ones, such as Watling Street and Fosse Way in Britain.

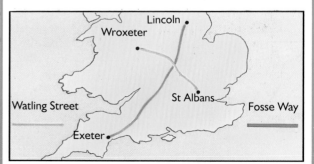

Lincoln

Wroxeter

Watling Street

St Albans

Fosse Way

Exeter

Flight path

Flight paths

Flying overcomes all the obstacles on land, but planes cannot fly just anywhere in the sky. They have to follow routes called flight paths. These are set at certain heights so that planes do not fly too close to each other.

Bridges called **aqueducts** carry canals across roads and other obstacles.

People cross water by ferry, bridge or tunnel.

Waterways

Rivers were the first waterways used for transport, but people could only travel along the natural path of the river. So, they built canals to reach major towns that were not on the riverside. Sea crossings also follow routes. Ports are linked by shipping lanes which avoid dangerous waters.

New, major roads may be built above other routes so that traffic flows freely.

Roads in marshy areas have extra foundations beneath them to stop them from sinking.

DID YOU KNOW?

• The longest bridge held up between two supports is the Humber Bridge in the UK, at 1,401m (4,626ft). The Akashi-Kaikyo Bridge in Japan, due to open in 1997, will be even longer, at 1,780m (5,839ft).
• The longest tunnel is the Seikan Rail Tunnel in Japan, measuring 53.85km (33.46 miles).
• The longest ship canal is the Suez Canal in Egypt. It measures 161.9km (100.6 miles).

Route through America

The Panama Canal saves ships a long journey around South America. It cuts through Central America, making a direct route between the Pacific and the Atlantic Oceans.

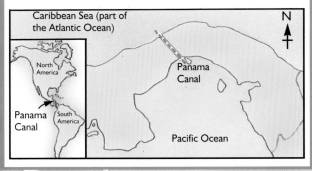

Caribbean Sea (part of the Atlantic Ocean)

N

North America

Panama Canal

Panama Canal

South America

Pacific Ocean

Stopping places

Points where routes meet and cross, such as towns, ports and airports, make good stopping places. They provide services* for travellers, such as shops and hotels.

Communication

In the 20th century, the speed of communication has increased enormously. Some people say that the world is shrinking because, as communication improves, it takes less and less time to get a message to the other side of the world. Quick communication makes it easier for people in different countries to organize business, sport, politics and many other events together.

These days, messages in the form of pictures, writing and sound can be sent electrically. Telephones, televisions, radios, fax machines and computers all work in this way. Electrical signals travel instantly along cables and through radio waves in the air, so people can receive messages as soon as they are sent. These two pages show some ways in which signals can be transmitted.

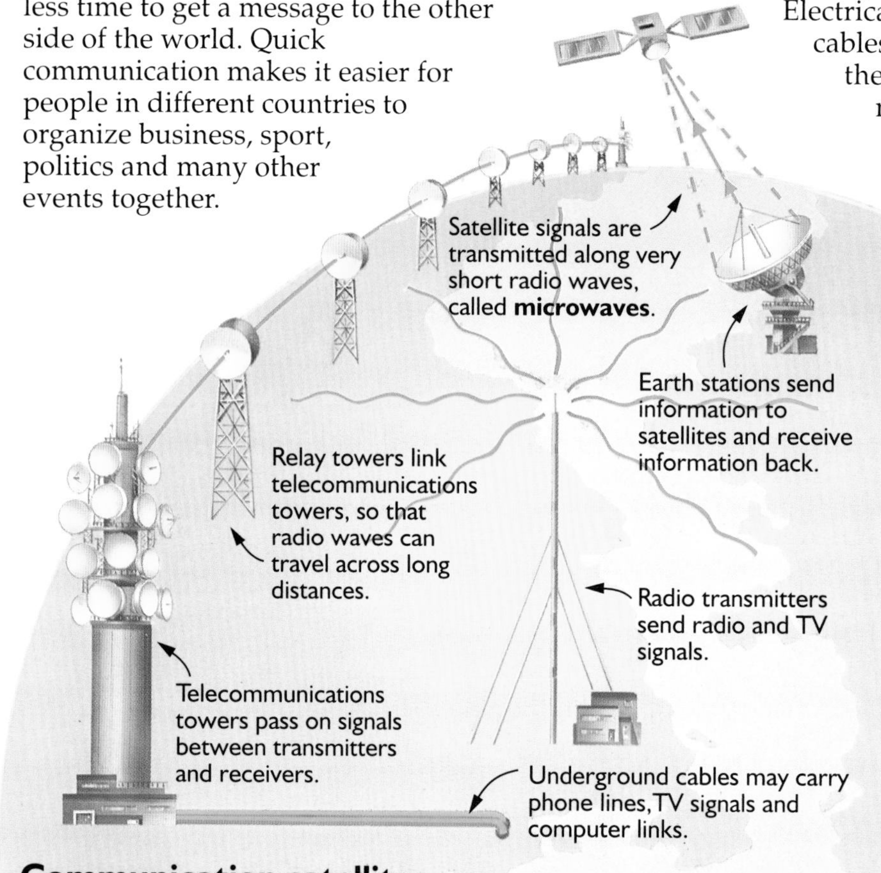

Satellite signals are transmitted along very short radio waves, called **microwaves**.

Earth stations send information to satellites and receive information back.

Relay towers link telecommunications towers, so that radio waves can travel across long distances.

Radio transmitters send radio and TV signals.

Telecommunications towers pass on signals between transmitters and receivers.

Underground cables may carry phone lines, TV signals and computer links.

DID YOU KNOW?

In 1912, an ocean liner, called the *Titanic*, sank in the Atlantic. The nearest ship had its radio switched off and did not hear the distress call, so many people died. After this disaster, it became law for all ships to carry radios and always listen for emergency calls.

The *Titanic*

Communication satellites

There are many satellites orbiting the Earth. Communication satellites carry TV programmes and phone calls. They travel at the same speed as the Earth, so they are always above the same patch of land. They are called **geostationary satellites**.

Big events, such as sports matches or rock concerts, are broadcast live by geostationary satellite, so that people around the world can watch them instantly as they happen. This picture shows how a live event is broadcast from one side of the world to the other.

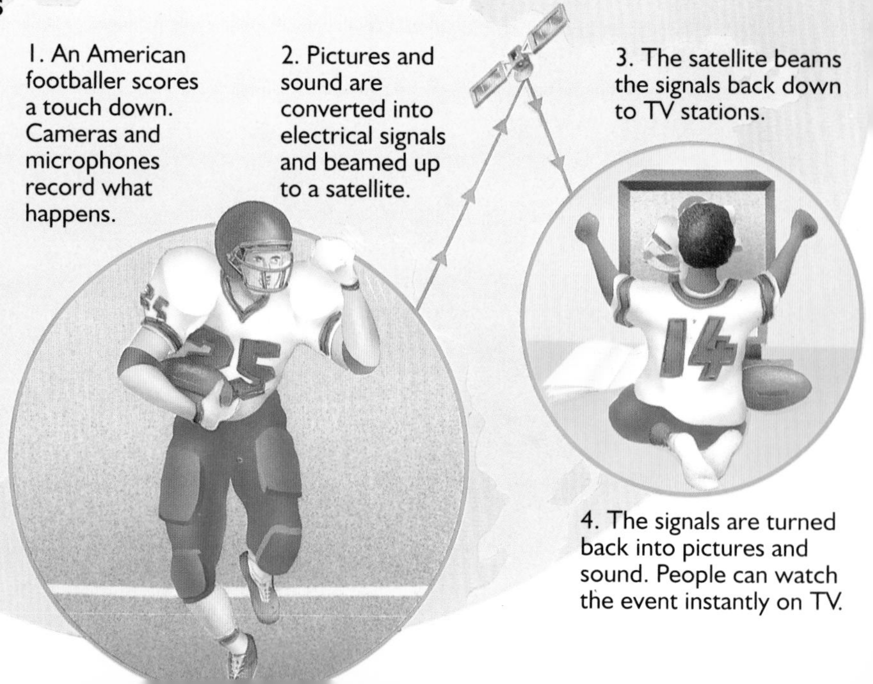

1. An American footballer scores a touch down. Cameras and microphones record what happens.

2. Pictures and sound are converted into electrical signals and beamed up to a satellite.

3. The satellite beams the signals back down to TV stations.

4. The signals are turned back into pictures and sound. People can watch the event instantly on TV.

84

Satellites watching Earth

Some satellites help scientists to know what is happening on Earth, by sending back information. These are called **observation satellites** and they orbit the Earth on different paths and at different speeds.

These satellites, such as the American LANDSAT, send back data, which can be turned into multi-coloured images of the Earth's surface. Some gather information about the weather, some look for changes on land and at sea, and others monitor changes in climate.

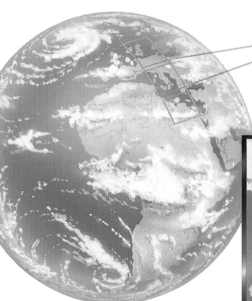

Satellites take overlapping pictures of the Earth's surface, so that nothing is missed out.

The satellite image on the right shows the temperature in Italy. The orange areas show where it is warmest and the yellow and green areas show where it is cooler.

Owning a phone

Although communication equipment is very advanced, there are still many places in the world where it is not easily available to ordinary people. For example, two thirds of the world's population do not have a phone in their house. The graph on the right shows the percentage of people who own a phone in some different countries.

% of people who own a phone

France 60%

Hungary 9%

Niger 0.15%

The history of signals

The earliest way to send a message, without taking it by hand, was to display a sign that could be seen from far away, such as smoke or fire, or by waving flags.

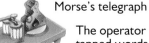

Morse's telegraph

The operator tapped words in code into the machine.

In the 1830s, Samuel Morse invented the **telegraph**, which sent electrical signals along a wire. People sent messages with a code of short and long bleeps, called **Morse Code**.

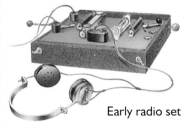

Early radio set

In 1901, the first radio message was sent across the Atlantic by a man called Marconi. He proved that radio waves can carry electrical signals.

Optical fibres are less than 1mm in diameter.

Today, information can be turned into light pulses as well as electrical signals. Tiny glass tubes called **optical fibres** carry light pulses. Each pair of optical fibres can carry 2,000 phone calls at any one time.

Resources

A **resource** is anything that people find useful. Almost everything in the natural world can be a resource, such as wind, water, rocks, metals, or even the countryside. Many of our natural resources are the raw materials* that are used in manufacturing.

However, materials only become a resource when people find a use for them. For example, rubber trees existed long before their sap, called latex, was used in manufacturing tyres or raincoats. Also, resources can only be used if reaching them does not cost more money than they are worth. People use tin much less than before because it has become too expensive to mine and aluminium can now be used instead.

Today, a bigger range of resources is being used because new technology helps the development of resources and new uses for them are discovered. However, it is possible that some resources may run out if they are overused.

Using resources

There are many different kinds of resources. Our most important ones are soil, wind, water and heat and light from the Sun. People use them to generate energy and grow food.

Minerals* are some of our most valuable raw materials. They are split into two groups: metals, including copper, zinc and lead; and non-metals, including oil, sand and silicon. Minerals are used in the building and chemical industries and some, such as fossil fuels*, are used to generate energy.

Forests are also valuable resources. Around two billion people use wood for heating and cooking. There is such demand for wood that many forests in developing countries* are being destroyed. Wood is also needed for building and manufacturing, for which there are two types of wood. Softwood is produced by quick-growing conifers* and hardwood is produced by slow-growing deciduous trees*.

Wood is not the only forest resource. Forests are the source of many raw materials, such as those used to make drugs. There may be thousands more plants and animals that will benefit people, which are still undiscovered in the world's forests.

Soil supports plant life, providing food for people and animals.

Copper is manufactured into items such as pipes and copper wire.

Sand is used in glass-making and building.

Drugs for heart disease come from plants in the foxglove, or *Digitalis*, family.

Oil is used as a fuel to make energy and in the chemical industry to make plastics.

Softwood is used in paper-making and for light building materials.

Latex for rubber manufacturing comes from tropical rubber trees.

Silicon comes from quartz rock. It is used to make electronic components.

Hardwood is used for furniture-making and strong building materials.

Tourists and the environment

As towns and cities grow faster than ever, scenery and wide-open spaces are becoming more and more valuable as a resource. Many people have more leisure time and often prefer to spend it in the countryside.

However, the countryside is threatened by the growth of tourism, as well as the growth of cities. Thousands of visitors can cause great damage to the environment and destroy wildlife habitats.

On the Mediterranean coast, vast areas have been taken up by hotels.

In Britain, many footpaths have been eroded by walkers.

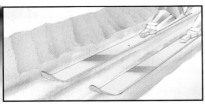

In the Alps and the Rocky Mountains, skiers have worn away mountain plants and caused landslides.

In the Philippines and on the Great Barrier Reef, coral has been destroyed by divers touching and treading on it.

Keeping the environment safe

Using resources changes the environment. Activities such as tourism, mining and road-building must be well planned. Planners make a study called an environmental assessment to show the possible effects of their project. If the project will be too damaging, then it has to change. For example, world banks no longer lend money to projects developing the Amazon Basin, due to environmental damage there.

Conservation and recycling

Many of our resources are non-renewable*, and will eventually run out. To make them last longer, people need to conserve (save) materials and recycle them as much as possible. Industries can play a major part in doing this. The picture below shows how one of them, the aluminium can manufacturing industry, has managed to increase its efficiency so that it saves both energy and materials.

Since 1955, the amount of energy used to produce one tonne (ton) of aluminium has fallen by 30%. This saves fuel.

Cans are now manufactured at least 25% thinner than in 1977, saving on raw materials.

Hydro-electric power (HEP)* is used to smelt* 61% of the world's aluminium. HEP is 57% more efficient than fossil fuels.

Many cans are now recycled. A recycled can uses only 5% of the energy needed to make one from aluminium ore*.

Recycled aluminium cans are 60% cheaper to make than non-reusable glass bottles and 75% cheaper than tin cans.

In Sweden, 70% of all cans are collected and recycled.

Individuals can also conserve and recycle materials. Always switching off appliances when they are not in use, using cars less and insulating the house better are all easy ways to save energy. Reusing materials, such as bottles and plastic bags saves resources and also cuts down on the amount of waste. Aluminium cans, paper, glass, and some plastics can all be recycled, which saves on fuels and materials.

*Hydro-electric power, 75; non-renewable, 74; ore, 72; smelting, 72.

Pollution

Pollution can damage the health of living things. Some kinds of pollution occur naturally, such as smoke from forest fires and volcanoes, or pollen from flowers. However, industries, farms, power stations, traffic and day-to-day living make a great deal more pollution by creating harmful substances, waste and noise.

Many animals are trapped and injured by litter, such as plastic can rings.

Fish are poisoned by metals in waste from industry. Animals that feed on fish are poisoned too.

Oil spilled from tanker ships sticks to birds and poisons them if they swallow it. Feathers covered in oil no longer keep birds warm, so they can die of cold.

Pollution on land and at sea

The landscape is polluted by waste. Large areas of land are taken up by ugly waste tips, which are created by the massive amounts of rubbish people make every day. Some people even dump litter in rivers or on the street.

Industrial waste, such as slag from coal mining, is also disposed of in huge dumps. Some waste is poisonous and may be buried beneath the ground to get rid of it. However, this is not always safe, as the poisons can leak out through underground streams. If water becomes polluted, it can easily affect a wide area, because rivers carry the pollution downstream. When it reaches the sea, currents spread it even further.

Chemicals from industry, and pesticides* and fertilizers* from farming are washed into rivers, where bacteria live off them. Bacteria use up the oxygen in water, so fish and water animals suffocate. In some places, untreated sewage is released into rivers and seas, causing disease in both animals and people.

Sewage and industrial waste may flow into rivers and the sea, where people sail and swim.

Cleaning up

So much pollution is being made that it is difficult to get rid of it safely. To keep the environment clean, governments can make laws to stop people from creating pollution. For example, it is illegal for oil tankers to pump out oil at sea. If they do, their captains may be fined.

Some famous cases of pollution have been caused by oil tankers, such as the *Exxon Valdez*, which crashed off the coast of Alaska in 1989.

Oil from the ship affected beaches, fishing-grounds and sea life. After an oil spill, experts must act quickly to rescue animals and clean up the sea and beaches.

There are several ways to clean up oil at sea. Peat or straw, which absorb oil, can be spread on it and scraped up. Or, floating barriers called booms can stop oil from spreading, so that it can then be sucked up by a tanker.

Air pollution

Industrial processes and motor vehicles all release substances into the air, such as lead, which can damage health. Some cities, for example Mexico City, are smothered by polluted air, called **smog**, which is bad to breathe. Loud noise is another kind of air pollution. It can cause deafness and other illnesses.

Acid rain

WIND

Acidic gases combine with moisture in the air and are carried away by the wind.

Acid rain falls. Animals and plants suffer.

Acid rain is a major form of air pollution. It is caused by acidic gases, such as nitrogen oxides and sulphur dioxide, which are released into the air by factory chimneys and vehicle exhaust pipes. These gases make moisture in the air up to a thousand times more acidic than usual.

Wind carries the moisture away, until it falls as acid rain, often in a nearby country. In Norway, 80% of rivers and streams either have, or soon will have, no life left in them. Ancient buildings, such as the Parthenon in Athens, are being worn away and forests in Europe and North America are dying.

The ozone layer

The ozone layer* is part of the atmosphere and protects us from the Sun's harmful rays. Chemicals called **CFCs** (chlorofluorocarbons), used in insulation material, aerosols and refrigerators attack ozone if they escape into the air. Holes are forming in the ozone layer and it will only return to its natural state if people stop using CFCs.

Hole in the ozone layer. It allows harmful rays to reach Earth.

Sun's rays

The Greenhouse Effect

The Earth is kept warm by the atmosphere which holds heat in. This process, called the **Greenhouse Effect**, happens naturally. However, many scientists agree that the Earth is getting warmer.

This warming is caused by an increase in certain gases, called **greenhouse gases**, in the air. These include carbon dioxide, CFCs and methane. They increase the atmosphere's ability to keep heat in. This diagram shows how the Greeenhouse Effect works.

1. Heat and light comes from the Sun.

2. Earth absorbs some heat and sends some back into the atmosphere.

3. Harmful greenhouse gases stop heat from escaping into space.

4. Some heat is kept in. Earth becomes warmer.

If the temperature on Earth increases too much, the weather and climate will change, harming animal and plant life. Ice at the Poles will melt, causing sea-levels to rise and land to be flooded.

What makes greenhouse gases?

Most greenhouse gases occur naturally, but now there is too much of them in the air. Carbon dioxide is produced by burning fuels and in industrial waste. Plants absorb carbon dioxide, but many trees are being cut down, so much less of it is used up. Methane is produced by some kinds of farming, such as cattle-raising and rice-growing, and from rotting waste. CFCs are not natural gases and are produced by the manufacturing industries.

*Ozone layer, 15.

Tomorrow's world

The world is changing faster than ever. It used to take years for new technology to be put into practice, but now it may take only months. The future is difficult to predict exactly, but many things which now seem strange may soon be part of everyday life.

Cities in the future

Cities in the future may be very different from today's cities. In order to create a warm environment where the weather is always pleasant, people may build cities in a see-through bubble, like the one in the picture. In Europe, there are already leisure parks enclosed in bubbles, so that visitors always get good weather. As land to build on becomes more scarce, people may even build cities under the sea or perhaps in space.

Each year, roads become busier and the air becomes more polluted* by petrol-driven vehicles. Future forms of transportation should be less harmful to the environment.

For some journeys, people may fly personal, one-seater aircraft or drive silent, electric cars. However, for regular journeys into and around the city, most people may travel on underground or overground light railways or monorails which run overhead.

Passenger aircraft for use on longer journeys may be able to take off and land vertically. This would save space on land, as these types of planes need only short runways. For very long journeys, people may even travel in low-level spacecraft.

Low-level spacecraft

Bubble city

Monorail

Electric car

The environment

The world population is expanding, so people will need more food, and more fresh water for drinking, farming and industry. It is now possible to have some control over the weather and the environment, and this may help to provide food and water for the future.

In low areas, such as the Netherlands, the sea has been drained away from coastal areas to make more land for building and farming. In dry areas, such as parts of Israel, it is possible to sprinkle the clouds with chemicals to make it rain on the crops. In the Middle East, factories take salt out of sea-water, to make it safe to drink. These methods may all be used more in the future, though people must be careful that they do not harm the environment.

Planes can sprinkle chemicals on clouds to make them rain.

*Pollution, 88.

City in space

Personal aircraft

Airport with short
runways, for planes
that take off vertically.

Scientists say that in the future, meals of vegetables and meat may be replaced by a diet of vitamin and mineral pills. However, people would probably not want to give up real food.

Communication

In the future, people will invent new ways of communication. People may own phones, called view-phones, which will have TV screens so that people can see, as well as hear, each other. It would be possible to have a view-phone meeting with people who were all in different places. Everyone would appear on the screen at once and be able to communicate with anyone else.

One day, we may even be able to invent machines that send tastes and smells, as we now send messages of sound and pictures.

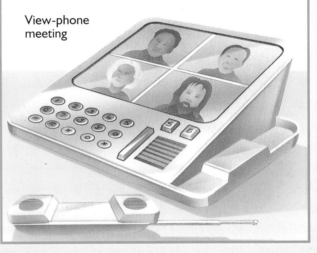

View-phone meeting

Energy

In the future, as fossil fuels* run out, we are likely to need new sources of energy. Scientists are working on many new ideas, such as **nuclear fusion**. This is the process of joining parts of atoms together to release massive amounts of energy.

Scientists are also developing a method of making power called **Ocean Thermal Energy Conversion (OTEC)**. This uses the difference in temperature between layers of tropical sea-water to boil a liquid into gas, which then drives a turbine and generates electricity.

A new lifestyle

As technology improves, our everyday lives may change. Many more jobs may be done by computers or robots. There will still be a need for workers, but jobs may be shared by more people. This means that people may have shorter working hours and more leisure time.

People also need to change their way of life so that they look after the Earth and waste less of its natural resources. If people want to preserve the Earth and its resources for future generations, they must use materials efficiently and reuse as much as possible.

*Fossil fuels, 74.

The world

Over 70% of the Earth's surface is covered by water. Most of it is contained in the four oceans: the Arctic, the Atlantic, the Indian and the Pacific. The total land area is around 150,000,000km² (58,000,000 square miles). It is divided into six continents — Asia, America, Africa, Europe, Antarctica and Australia.

The world is split up into different countries. There are currently 185 countries, but this number is always changing as some countries join together and others split up to form separate states.

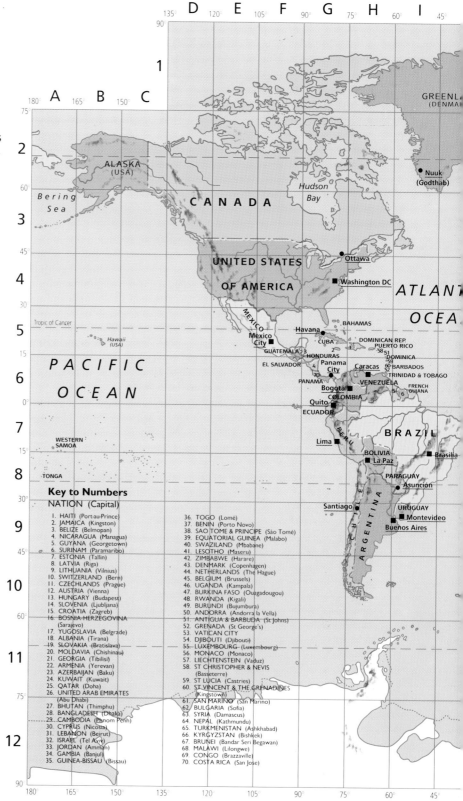

Key

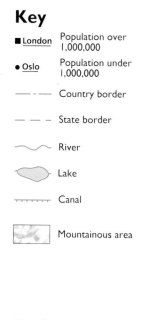

- ■ London — Population over 1,000,000
- ● Oslo — Population under 1,000,000
- – – – Country border
- — — State border
- ～～ River
- Lake
- ┬┬┬ Canal
- Mountainous area

Key to Numbers
NATION (Capital)

1. HAITI (Port-au-Prince)
2. JAMAICA (Kingston)
3. BELIZE (Belmopan)
4. NICARAGUA (Managua)
5. GUYANA (Georgetown)
6. SURINAM (Paramaribo)
7. ESTONIA (Tallin)
8. LATVIA (Riga)
9. LITHUANIA (Vilnius)
10. SWITZERLAND (Bern)
11. CZECHLANDS (Prague)
12. AUSTRIA (Vienna)
13. HUNGARY (Budapest)
14. SLOVENIA (Ljubljana)
15. CROATIA (Zagreb)
16. BOSNIA-HERZEGOVINA (Sarajevo)
17. YUGOSLAVIA (Belgrade)
18. ALBANIA (Tirana)
19. SLOVAKIA (Bratislava)
20. MOLDAVIA (Chishinau)
21. GEORGIA (Tibilisi)
22. ARMENIA (Yerevan)
23. AZERBAIJAN (Baku)
24. KUWAIT (Kuwait)
25. QATAR (Doha)
26. UNITED ARAB EMIRATES (Abu Dhabi)
27. BHUTAN (Thimphu)
28. BANGLADESH (Dhaka)
29. CAMBODIA (Phnom Penh)
30. CYPRUS (Nicosia)
31. LEBANON (Beirut)
32. ISRAEL (Tel Aviv)
33. JORDAN (Amman)
34. GAMBIA (Banjul)
35. GUINEA-BISSAU (Bissau)

36. TOGO (Lomé)
37. BENIN (Porto Novo)
38. SAO TOME & PRINCIPE (São Tomé)
39. EQUATORIAL GUINEA (Malabo)
40. SWAZILAND (Mbabane)
41. LESOTHO (Maseru)
42. ZIMBABWE (Harare)
43. DENMARK (Copenhagen)
44. NETHERLANDS (The Hague)
45. BELGIUM (Brussels)
46. UGANDA (Kampala)
47. BURKINA FASO (Ouagadougou)
48. RWANDA (Kigali)
49. BURUNDI (Bujumbura)
50. ANDORRA (Andorra la Vella)
51. ANTIGUA & BARBUDA (St Johns)
52. GRENADA (St George's)
53. VATICAN CITY
54. DJIBOUTI (Djibouti)
55. LUXEMBOURG (Luxembourg)
56. MONACO (Monaco)
57. LIECHTENSTEIN (Vaduz)
58. ST CHRISTOPHER & NEVIS (Basseterre)
59. ST LUCIA (Castries)
60. ST VINCENT & THE GRENADINES (Kingstown)
61. SAN MARINO (San Marino)
62. BULGARIA (Sofia)
63. SYRIA (Damascus)
64. NEPAL (Kathmundu)
65. TURKMENISTAN (Ashkhabad)
66. KYRGYZSTAN (Bishkek)
67. BRUNEI (Bandar Seri Begawan)
68. MALAWI (Lilongwe)
69. CONGO (Brazzaville)
70. COSTA RICA (San Jose)

Scale

Kilometres:

0 ... 500

Miles:
0 ... 500 ... 1000

East of
Greenwich
t of
wich
L   M   N   O   P   Q   R   S   T   U   V   W
0°   15°   30°   45°   60°   75°   90°   105°   120°   135°   150°   165°
90°

ARCTIC OCEAN

X   Y   180°   165°

75°

*Barents
Sea*

RUSSIAN FEDERATION

Arctic Circle

AND
avik

60°

■ Helsinki

Oslo ●   ■ Stockholm
■ Berlin   ■ Warsaw
7 8
■ Moscow

UNITED
KINGDOM
AND
ublin
London
44

BELORUSSIA
POLAND   UKRAINE
■ Kiev

KAZAKHSTAN

Ulan Bator ●
MONGOLIA

N KOREA
Pyŏngyang ●
S KOREA   Seoul ●

JAPAN
■ Tōkyō

PACIFIC
OCEAN

45°

Paris
FRANCE
56   61
Madrid   Tunis
Algiers
Rabat
MOROCCO

GER-
MANY
45
ITALY
14
Rome
18
GREECE
Athens
9
MALTA
TUNISIA

11
ROMANIA   Bucharest
13   13
17   62
16
Black Sea

71

Tashkent ■
UZBEKISTAN
65
TAJIKISTAN
Dushanbe ■
AFGHANISTAN
Kabul ●
Islamabad ■

Alma-Ata ●

■ Ankara
TURKEY   Tehran ●
30   63
33   IRAQ
32   Baghdad
34
IRAN

66

JAMMU
KASHMIR

CHINA

Beijing ●

Tai-Pei ●
TAIWAN

30°

SPAIN
90
PORTUGAL
on

60
58

61

ALGERIA   LIBYA

Cairo ●
EGYPT

SAUDI
Riyadh ●
ARABIA

BAHRAIN
26
● Muscat
OMAN

New Delhi ■
64   ▪ 27
28

INDIA

MYANMAR
(BURMA)
Rangoon ●

Hanoi ■

Tropic of Cancer

Tropic of Cancer

RITANIA
MALI

NIGER   CHAD
Niamey ●

Khartoum ●
SUDAN   San'a
REP OF
YEMEN

*Arabian
Sea*

● Colombo
SRI LANKA

Bangkok ■
THAILAND
29

LAOS
VIETNAM
Manila ■
PHILIPPINES

15°

NE
GAL
Bamako ●
GUINEA
37
ova
Accra
Yamous-
ssoukro

N'Djamena ●
NIGERIA
Abuja ●
CAMEROON

CENTRAL
AFRICAN REPUBLIC
Bangui ●
Yaoundé
38   39
69

Addis Ababa ■
ETHIOPIA

SOMALIA
Mogadishu ■

Kuala
Lumpur ■
MALAYSIA
67

Equator

IVORY
COAST
Libreville ●
GABON

46
48
49

KENYA
Nairobi ●

SEYCHELLES

MALDIVES

Jakarta ■
INDONESIA

PAPUA NEW
GUINEA

NAURU

SOLOMON
ISLANDS
Honiara ■
TUVALU

KIRIBATI

0°

Luanda ●

Kinshasa ●
ZAIRE

TANZANIA
Dodoma ●

COMOROS

Port Moresby ●

VANUATU

15°

ANGOLA
ZAMBIA
Lusaka ●
68
NAMIBIA
42
Gaborone ●
BOTSWANA

MADAGASCAR
Antananarivo ■
MOZAMBIQUE

Port Louis ●
MAURITIUS

INDIAN

AUSTRALIA

Suva ■   FIJI

Tropic
of Capricorn

Walvis Bay (S.A.)
Windhoek
SOUTH
AFRICA
41

Pretoria ●   Maputo ■

OCEAN

30°

NEW
ZEALAND

● Canberra

Wellington ■

45°

TASMANIA

60°

Antarctic Circle

N

ANTARCTICA

W   E

75°

S

90°

North America

America is the second biggest continent. It is made up of three main areas, North, Central and South America. North America, shown here, covers 19,343,000km² (7,468,000 square miles). There are only two countries in North America — the United States of America and Canada. Canada is the largest country in the world. Central and South America are shown on pages 96-97.

Key

America are shown on pages 96-97.

<u>Ottawa</u>	Capital city
■ Phoenix	Population over 1,000,000
● Billings	Population 100,000 - 1,000,000
⊙ Fairbanks	Population under 100,000
— ‧ —	Country border
— — —	State border

	River
	Lake
	Canal
	Mountainous area
McKinley ▲ 6194 (20316)	Mountain peak - height in metres (feet)

Scale

Kilometres:

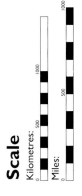

0   500   1000

Miles:

0   500   1000

Key to numbers

1. MASSACHUSETTS
2. CONNECTICUT

National flags

Canada

United States
of America

95

Central and South America

Central and South America are part of the continent America, which is the second biggest continent in the world. Together, they cover 23,617,000km² (9,119,000 square miles). The Amazon forest, which is the biggest area of rainforest in the world, is in South America. This area is also the largest river basin in the world.

Key

Quito

■ Recife

● São José

⊙ Tomatlán

Capital city

Population over 1,000,000

Population 100,000 - 1,000,000

Population under 100,000

Country border

State border

River

Lake

Canal

Mountainous area

▲ Cotopaxi 5896 (19338)   Mountain peak - height in metres (feet)

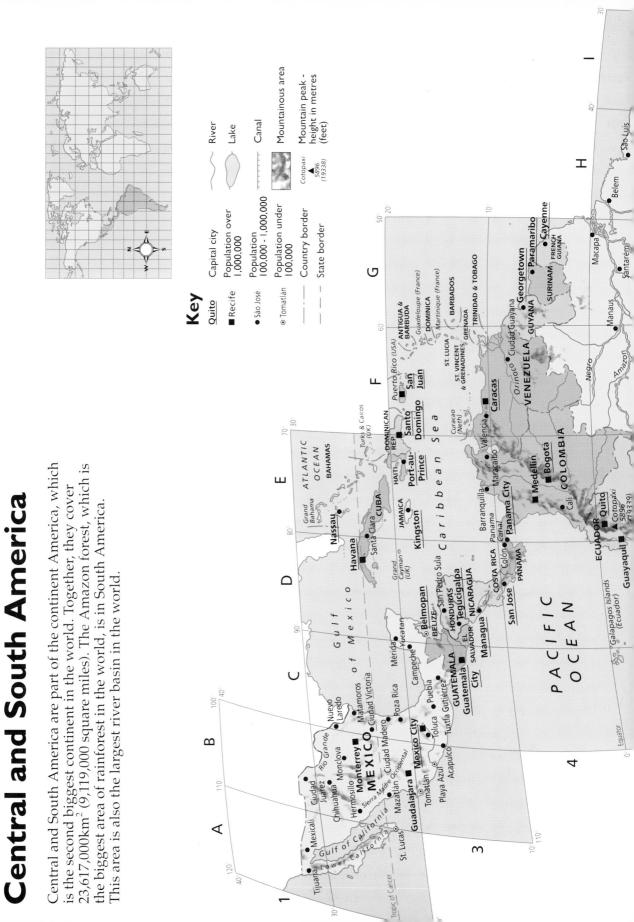

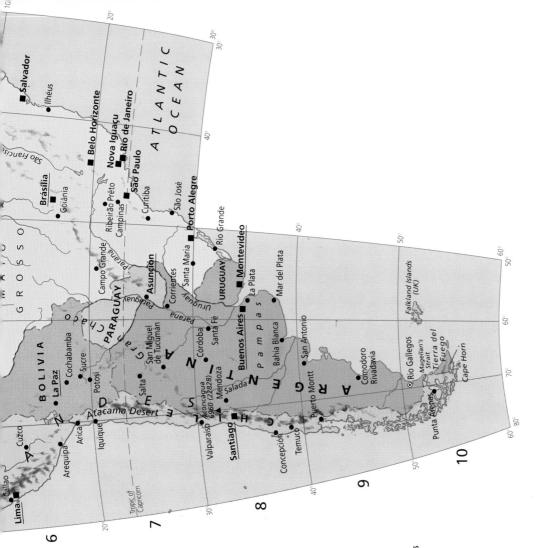

ATLANTIC OCEAN

National flags

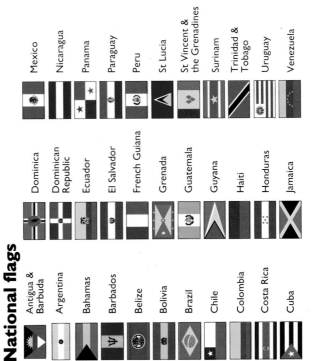

Antigua & Barbuda	Dominica	Mexico
Argentina	Dominican Republic	Nicaragua
Bahamas	Ecuador	Panama
Barbados	El Salvador	Paraguay
Belize	French Guiana	Peru
Bolivia	Grenada	St Lucia
Brazil	Guatemala	St Vincent & the Grenadines
Chile	Guyana	Surinam
Colombia	Haiti	Trinidad & Tobago
Costa Rica	Honduras	Uruguay
Cuba	Jamaica	Venezuela

Scale

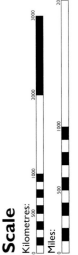

Kilometres:
0   500   1000   2000   3000

Miles:
0   500   1000   2000

Africa

Africa is the third biggest continent, covering 30,335,000km² (11,712,000 square miles). The Nile, which is the longest river in the world, runs through Africa. The Sahara, which is the biggest desert in the world, is also in Africa.

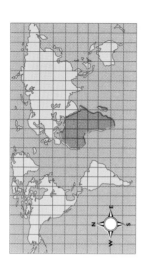

Key

Nairobi	Capital city
■ Abidjan	Population over 1,000,000
● Suez	Population 100,000 - 1,000,000
⊙ Kayes	Population under 100,000
—·—·—	Country border
— — —	State border
〰	River
⬭	Lake
	Canal
	Mountainous area
▲ Kilimanjaro 5895 (19335)	Mountain peak - height in metres (feet)

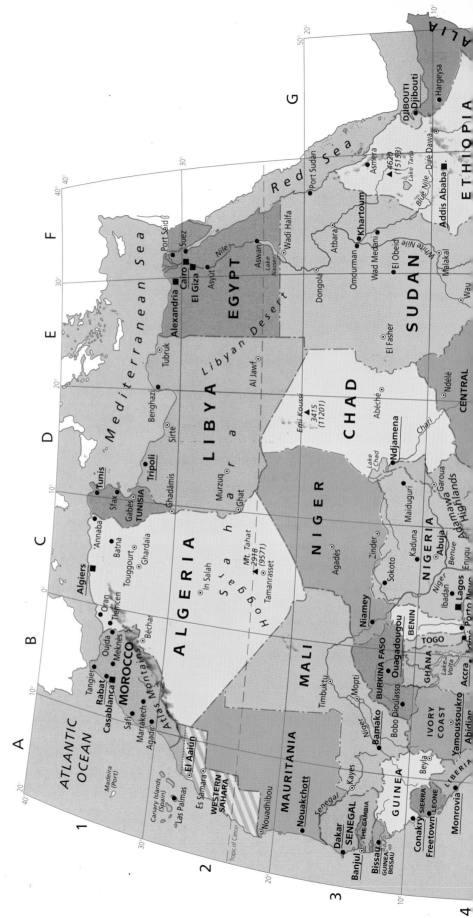

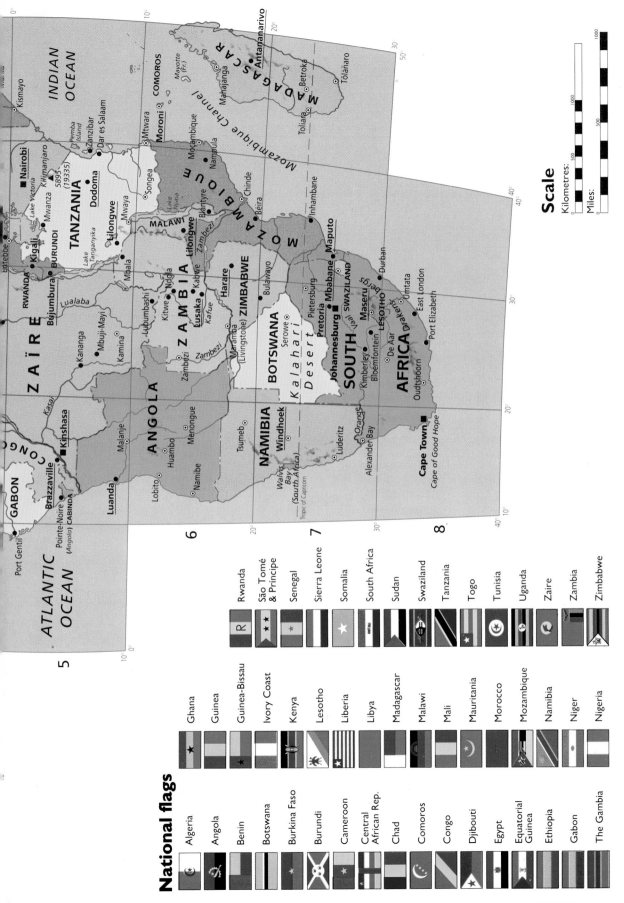

National flags

Europe

Europe is the region that stretches from Britain in the west to the Ural Mountains of Russia in the east. It is the fourth largest continent, covering 10,498,000km^2 (4,052,000 square miles). It is the most densely populated continent, where the towns and cities are crowded together more than anywhere else.

National flags

	Albania		Greece		Poland
	Andorra		Hungary		Portugal
	Austria		Iceland		Romania
	Belgium		Ireland		Slovakia
	Bosnia - Herzegovina		Italy		Slovenia
	Bulgaria		Latvia		Spain
	Croatia		Liechtenstein		Sweden
	Cyprus		Lithuania		Switzerland
	Czechlands		Luxembourg		Turkey
	Denmark		Malta		United Kingdom
	Estonia		Monaco		Yugoslavia
	Finland		Netherlands		
	France		Norway		
	Georgia				
	Germany				

Scale

Kilometres:
0 — 500

Miles:
0 — 500

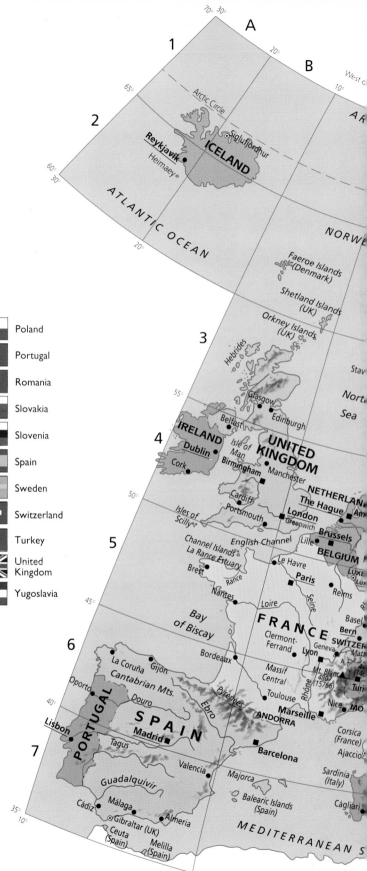

100

N

10°

E

F

G

40° 70°

N

S

W E

Hammerfest

30°

Tromso

Narvik

65°

Lulea

Kemi

Oulu

60°

Trondheim

S W E D E N

F I N L A N D

Umeå

Gulf of Bothnia

Vaasa

Varkaus

Tampere

Turku

Helsinki

55°

Glåma

Oslo

Västerås

Aland Is.
(Finland)

Gulf of Finland

Tallinn

Lake
Vänern

Stockholm

ESTONIA

Pskov

Lake
Vättern

Riga

Jönköping

Gotland

Baltic Sea

LATVIA

Daugavpils

RK

agen

Klaipeda

LITHUANIA

Malmö

Bornholm
(Denmark)

PART OF
RUSSIAN
FEDERATION

Vilnius

50°

urg

Gdańsk

lin

POLAND

Poznan

Oder

Vistula

Łódź

Warsaw

den

Wrocław

Kraków

THE
CZECHLANDS

SLOVAKIA

Brno

Carpathians

Prut

50° 45°

Vienna

Bratislava

Košice

AUSTRIA

Danube

Budapest

H

Graz

HUNGARY

Cluj-
Napoca

ana

SLOVENIA

Zagreb

ROMANIA

40°

CROATIA

Sava

Drava

Caucasus Mts.

GEORGIA

Tbilisi

BOSNIA -
HERZEGOVINA

Belgrade

Craiova

Bucharest

Black Sea

Split

Danube

Mt. Ararat

Adriatic Sea

Sarajevo

YUGOSLAVIA

BULGARIA

5123
(16803)

Podgorica

Sofia

Balkan Mts.

Samsun

Van
Gölü

Tirana

ALBANIA

Skopje

Istanbul

Izmit

T U R K E Y

35°

Thessaloniki

Bursa

Ankara

Elâzig

50°

ermo

GREECE

Aegean
Sea

Konya

Kayseri

Firat

Urfa

ITALY

Reggio di
Calabria

Ionian
Sea

Pátrai

Izmir

Mersin

an Sea

Athens

Antalya

40°

Valletta

Rhodes
(Greece)

CYPRUS

cily

Crete
(Greece)

30°

Key

Commonwealth of Independent States

The Commonwealth of Independent States (CIS) is a group of countries which are joined together for trade purposes, covering northern Asia and part of eastern Europe. They used to be part of the former Soviet Union. The Russian Federation is the largest of these countries and is the second largest country in the world.

Key

<u>Moscow</u>	Capital city
■Donetsk	Population over 1,000,000
●Bratsk	Population 100,000 - 1,000,000
⊙Suntar	Population under 100,000
— · —	Country border
— — —	State border
∿	River
⬭	Lake
⊦⊦⊦⊦⊦	Canal
▨	Mountainous area
Elbrus ▲ 5633 (18476)	Mountain peak - height in metres (feet)

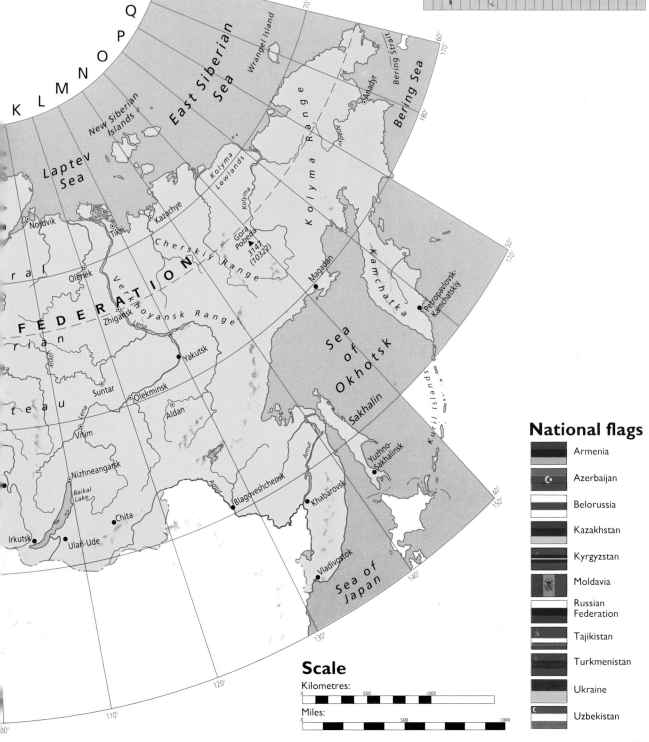

R
Q
P
O
N
M
L
K

80°

East Siberian Sea

70°

Wrangel Island

60°

Bering Strait

170°

Bering Sea

New Siberian Islands

Laptev Sea

Kolyma Lowlands

Kolyma Range

Anadyr

180°

Kolyma

Anadyr

Nordvik

Tiksi

Kazachye

Kolyma

Cherskiy Range

Gora Pobeda
3147
(10322)

Kamchatka

50°

Petropavlovsk-Kamchatskiy

Olenek

F E D E R A T I O N

Verkhoyansk Range

Zhigansk

Lena

Magadan

170°

Sea
of
Okhotsk

Yakutsk

Suntar

Olekminsk

Aldan

Sakhalin

40°

Vitim

Lena

Nizhneangarsk

Baikal
Lake

Amur

Yuzhno-Sakhalinsk

150°

Chita

Blagoveshchensk

Khabarovsk

Kuril Islands

Irkutsk

Ulan-Ude

Vladivostok

140°

Sea of
Japan

130°

120°

110°

100°

National flags

Armenia

Azerbaijan

Belorussia

Kazakhstan

Kyrgyzstan

Moldavia

Russian
Federation

Tajikistan

Turkmenistan

Ukraine

Uzbekistan

Scale

Kilometres:

0   500   1000

Miles:

0   500   1000

Southern Asia and the Middle East

Asia is the largest continent, covering 43,608,000km² (16,833,000 square miles). Its countries include China, which has the world's largest population. The Himalayas are the world's tallest mountains, of which the hightest is Mount Everest. The Middle East is the area surrounding the Gulf.

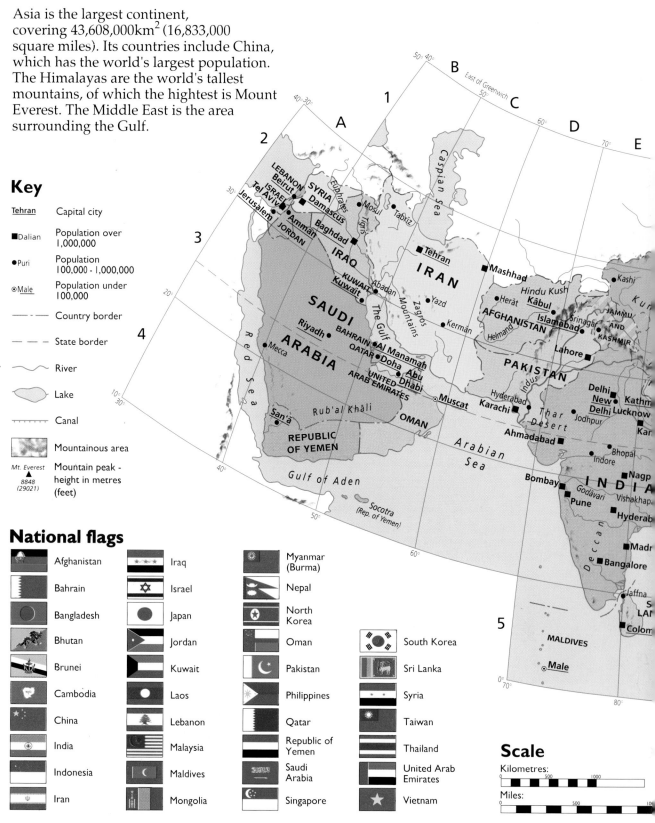

Key

<u>Tehran</u>	Capital city
■Dalian	Population over 1,000,000
●Puri	Population 100,000 - 1,000,000
◎<u>Male</u>	Population under 100,000
— · — · —	Country border
— — —	State border
⌇⌇	River
⬭	Lake
⊢⊢⊢⊢	Canal
	Mountainous area
Mt. Everest ▲ 8848 (29021)	Mountain peak - height in metres (feet)

National flags

	Afghanistan		Iraq		Myanmar (Burma)		
	Bahrain		Israel		Nepal		
	Bangladesh		Japan		North Korea		South Korea
	Bhutan		Jordan		Oman		Sri Lanka
	Brunei		Kuwait		Pakistan		Syria
	Cambodia		Laos		Philippines		Taiwan
	China		Lebanon		Qatar		Thailand
	India		Malaysia		Republic of Yemen		United Arab Emirates
	Indonesia		Maldives		Saudi Arabia		
	Iran		Mongolia		Singapore		Vietnam

Scale

Kilometres:
0 ... 500 ... 1000

Miles:
0 ... 500 ... 100

Sapporo ■ Hokkaido

Amur

HARBIN ■

NORTH KOREA

Sea

Japan

of

Japan

JAPAN

Honshū

Fushun ■

MONGOLIA

Ulan Bator ●

Gobi Desert

Nan Shan

Tangshan

Pyŏngyang

Seoul

SOUTH
KOREA

Tōkyō ■

Yokohama ■

Kyōto

Ōsaka

Pusan

Kyūshū

Fukuoka ■

Tropic of Cancer

Beijing ■

Dalian ■

Tianjin ■

Qingdao ■

Huang He

Taiyuan ■

Lanzhou ■

Zhengzhou ■

Xi'an

Shanghai ■

East
China
Sea

Ryukyu Islands

Wuhan ■

Hangzhou ■

Chengdu ■

Chang Jiang

Nanchang ■

Chongqing ■

Changsha ■

Fuzhou ■

Taipei ■

TAIWAN

Guiyang ■

Kunming ■

Wuzhou ●

Guangzhou ■

Macau
(Portugal)

Hong Kong
(UK)

PACIFIC
OCEAN

Lhasa ●

Plateau
of
Tibet

H

Thimphu ●

BHUTAN

Cherrapunji

Brahmaputra

BANGLADESH

Dhaka ■

Chittagong ■

MYANMAR
(BURMA)

Irrawaddy

Hanoi ■

Xi Jiang

Chang Jiang

C H I N A

N

Luzon

Quezon City ■

Manila ■

PHILIPPINES

Vientiane ■

LAOS

VIETNAM

Da Nang

Mekong

South
China
Sea

Cebu ●

Mindanao

Davao ●

THAILAND

Rangoon ■

Bangkok ■

CAMBODIA

Phnom
Penh ●

Ho Chi
Minh City ■

Gulf
of
Thailand

Spratly
Islands

Sulu
Sea

Andaman
&
Nicobar Is.
(India)

Bay
of
Bengal

MALAYSIA

Bandar Seri
Begawan ◉

BRUNEI

Celebes
Sea

Maluku

Jayapura

New
Guinea

Equator

INDIAN
OCEAN

George Town ●

Kuching ●

Balikpapan ●

Palu ●

Seram

Medan ■

Kuala
Lumpur ●

SINGAPORE ■

Borneo

Sulawesi

I N D O N E S I A

Arafura
Sea

Sumatra

Padang ●

Ujung
Pandang ●

Jakarta ■

Semarang ■

Java

Surabaya ■

Bali

Flores

Sumba

Timor

Australasia and Oceania

Australasia is the area south-east of Asia, which includes Australia, New Zealand, Papua New Guinea and their surrounding islands. Oceania is the name given to all the other islands in the Pacific Ocean. Australia itself is the smallest continent in the world, covering 7,682,300km² (2,966,150 square miles).

Key

<u>Canberra</u>	Capital city
■Brisbane	Population over 1,000,000
●Perth	Population 100,000 - 1,000,000
⊙Albany	Population under 100,000
— · —	Country border
— —	State border
～～	River
⬭	Lake
⊥⊥⊥⊥	Canal
▨	Mountainous area
Ayers Rock ▲ 867 (2843)	Mountain peak - height in metres (feet)

National flags

Australia	
Fiji	
Kiribati	
Nauru	
New Zealand	
Papua New Guinea	

Solomon Islands	
Tonga	
Tuvalu	
Vanuatu	
Western Samoa	

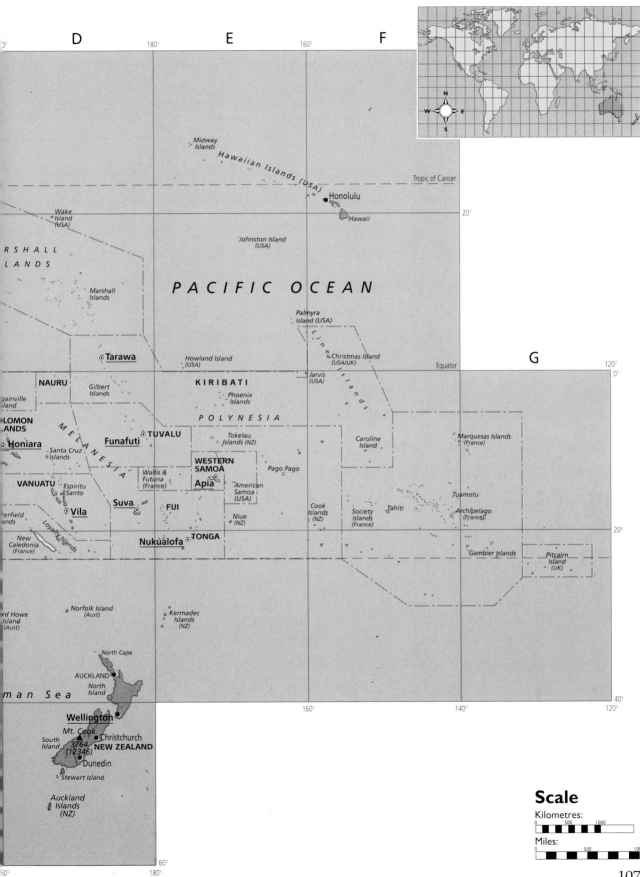

D · E · 180° · 160° · F

Midway Islands

Hawaiian Islands (USA)

Tropic of Cancer

Honolulu

Wake Island (USA)

20°

Hawaii

Johnston Island (USA)

MARSHALL ISLANDS

Marshall Islands

PACIFIC OCEAN

Palmyra Island (USA)

Tarawa

Howland Island (USA)

Christmas Island (USA/UK)

Equator

G

120° 0°

NAURU

Gilbert Islands

KIRIBATI

Jarvis (USA)

Bougainville Island

Phoenix Islands

POLYNESIA

SOLOMON ISLANDS

M E L A N E S I A

Honiara

Santa Cruz Islands

Funafuti · TUVALU

Tokelau Islands (NZ)

Caroline Island

Marquesas Islands (France)

WESTERN SAMOA

Pago Pago

VANUATU

Espiritu Santo

Wallis & Futuna (France)

Apia

American Samoa (USA)

Tuamotu Archipelago (France)

Vila

Suva

FIJI

Niue (NZ)

Cook Islands (NZ)

Society Islands (France)

Tahiti

20°

Loyalty Islands

Waterfield Islands

New Caledonia (France)

Nukualofa · TONGA

Gambier Islands

Pitcairn Island (UK)

Lord Howe Island (Aust)

Norfolk Island (Aust)

Kermadec Islands (NZ)

man Sea

North Cape

AUCKLAND

North Island

40°

160° · 140° · 120°

Wellington

Mt. Cook

South Island

3764 (12346)

Christchurch

NEW ZEALAND

Dunedin

Stewart Island

Auckland Islands (NZ)

60°

180°

Scale

Kilometres:
0 · 500 · 1000

Miles:
0 · 500 · 1000

The polar world

The Arctic (around the North Pole) and
Antarctica (around the South Pole) are both
covered in ice. Antarctica is the second
smallest continent, covering 13,340,000km^2
(5,150,000 square miles). Many different
countries claim parts of its land. In the Arctic,
there is no land beneath the ice, only sea.

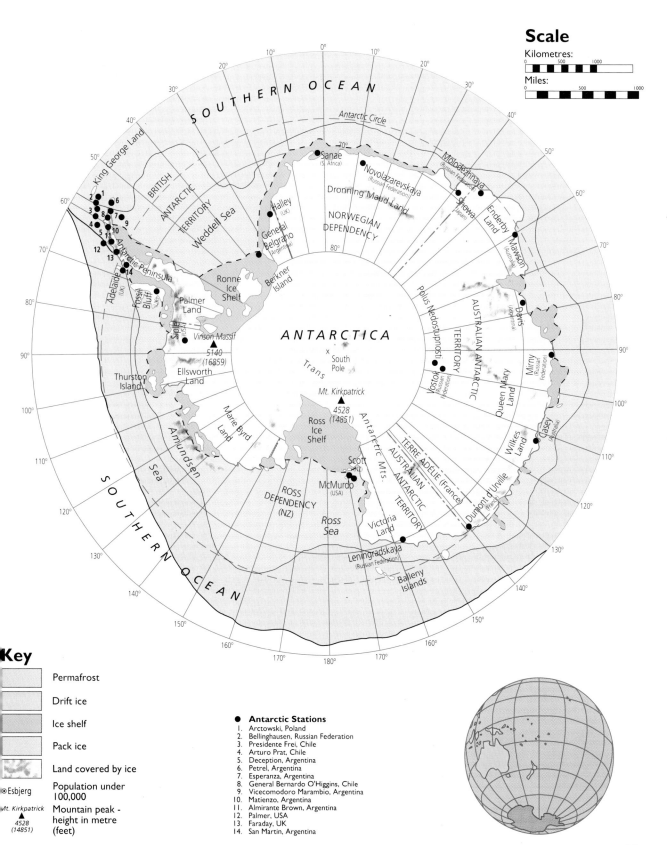

Scale

Kilometres:

Miles:

SOUTHERN OCEAN

Antarctic Circle

Sanae *(S. Africa)*

Molodezhnaya *(Russian Federation)*

Novolazarevskaya *(Russian Federation)*

Dronning Maud Land

Showa *(Japan)*

Enderby Land

Mawson *(Australia)*

King George Land

BRITISH ANTARCTIC TERRITORY

Weddell Sea

Halley *(UK)*

General Belgrano *(Argentina)*

NORWEGIAN DEPENDENCY

Berkner Island

Ronne Ice Shelf

Polus Nedostupnosti *(Argentina)*

AUSTRALIAN ANTARCTIC TERRITORY

Davis *(Australia)*

Antarctic Peninsula

Adelaide *(UK)*

Fossil Bluff *(UK)*

Palmer Land

ANTARCTICA

South Pole

Trans

Mirny *(Russian Federation)*

Queen Mary Land

Sple *(USA)*

Vinson Massif
▲
5140
(16859)

Ellsworth Land

Vostok *(Russian Federation)*

Thurston Island

Mt. Kirkpatrick
▲
4528
(14851)

Ross Ice Shelf

Antarctic Mts.

Casey *(Australia)*

Wilkes Land

Marie Byrd Land

Amundsen Sea

Scott *(NZ)*

McMurdo *(USA)*

TERRE ADELIE (France)

AUSTRALIAN ANTARCTIC TERRITORY

Dumont d'Urville *(France)*

ROSS DEPENDENCY (NZ)

Ross Sea

Victoria Land

SOUTHERN OCEAN

Leningradskaya *(Russian Federation)*

Balleny Islands

Key

	Permafrost
	Drift ice
	Ice shelf
	Pack ice
	Land covered by ice
⊚Esbjerg	Population under 100,000
Mt. Kirkpatrick ▲ 4528 (14851)	Mountain peak - height in metre (feet)

● Antarctic Stations

1. Arctowski, Poland
2. Bellinghausen, Russian Federation
3. Presidente Frei, Chile
4. Arturo Prat, Chile
5. Deception, Argentina
6. Petrel, Argentina
7. Esperanza, Argentina
8. General Bernardo O'Higgins, Chile
9. Vicecomodoro Marambio, Argentina
10. Matienzo, Argentina
11. Almirante Brown, Argentina
12. Palmer, USA
13. Faraday, UK
14. San Martin, Argentina

World facts

Our Solar System

Planet	Diameter in km (miles)		Distance from Sun in millions of km (miles)		Number of moons
Mercury	4,878	(3,029)	58	(36)	0
Venus	12,103	(7,516)	108	(67)	0
Earth	12,756	(7,921)	150	(93)	1
Mars	6,794	(4,219)	228	(141)	2
Jupiter	143,800	(88,700)	778	(483)	16
Saturn	120,000	(74,000)	1,427	(886)	17
Uranus	52,400	(32,500)	2,870	(1,782)	15
Neptune	49,400	(30,700)	4,497	(2,792)	8
Pluto	1,100	(680)	5,900	(3,700)	1

Phases of the Moon

As the Moon moves around the Earth, different parts of it are lit up by the Sun, so that it looks as if the Moon is changing shape. It seems to wax and wane (grow and shrink), depending on its position, or **phase**. This diagram shows the phases of the Moon and what the Moon looks like from Earth.

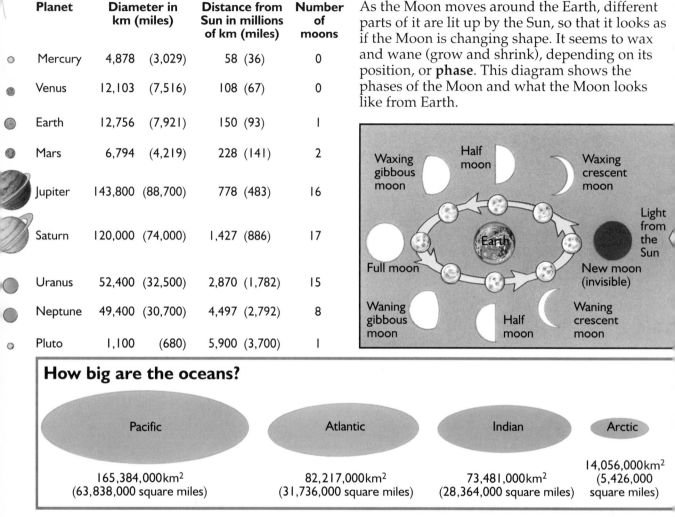

How big are the oceans?

Pacific
165,384,000km² (63,838,000 square miles)

Atlantic
82,217,000km² (31,736,000 square miles)

Indian
73,481,000km² (28,364,000 square miles)

Arctic
14,056,000km² (5,426,000 square miles)

Longest rivers

Nile, Africa	6,695km (4,160 miles)
Amazon, South America	6,516km (4,050 miles)
Yangtze (Chang Jiang); Asia	6,380km (3,965 miles)
Mississippi-Missouri, North America	6,019km (3,740 miles)
Ob -Irtysh, Asia	5,570km (3,460 miles)
Yenisey-Angara, Asia	5,550km (3,450 miles)
Huang He (Yellow River), Asia	5,464km (3,395 miles)
Zaire (Congo), Africa	4,667km (2,900 miles)
Paranà, South America	4,500km (2,800 miles)
Mekong, Asia	4,425km (2,750 miles)

Highest mountains

The world's highest mountains are all in the Himalayas in Asia. This diagram shows the highest mountain in each continent.

Mount Everest, Asia	8,848m (29,028ft)
Aconcagua, South America	6,960m (22,834ft)
McKinley, North America	6,194m (20,320ft)
Mount Kilimanjaro, Africa	5,895m (19,340ft)
Elbrus, Europe	5,642m (18,510ft)
Vinson Massif, Antarctica	5,140m (16,860ft)
Mount Wilhelm, Australasia	4,694m (15,400ft)

The world's biggest cities

City	Population
Mexico City, Mexico	18,748,000
New York, USA	16,121,000
Tokyo/Yokohama, Japan	14,804,000
Los Angeles, USA	11,498,000
São Paulo, Brazil	10,099,000
Buenos Aires, Argentina	9,968,000
Seoul, South Korea	9,639,000
Calcutta, India	9,194,000
Moscow, Russia	8,967,000
Paris, France	8,707,000

Famous earthquakes

There are two different scales for measuring earthquakes – the Richter Scale and the Mercalli Scale. You can find out about these on page 18. Below are six famous earthquakes that have happened within the last century.

Date	Earthquake	Richter Scale	Mercalli Scale
1906	San Fransisco, USA	8.3	10
1960	Agadir, Morocco	5.8	8
1963	Skopje, Yugoslavia	6.0	8
1964	Anchorage, Alaska, USA	7.5	9
1976	Tangshan, China	8.5	11
1985	Mexico City, Mexico	8.1	10

The climates

These graphs show what the climate is like in different areas of the world. The top lines of the coloured areas give an example of the average temperature (shown on the left-hand scale), in each month of the year. The bar charts give the average rainfall (shown on the right-hand scale).

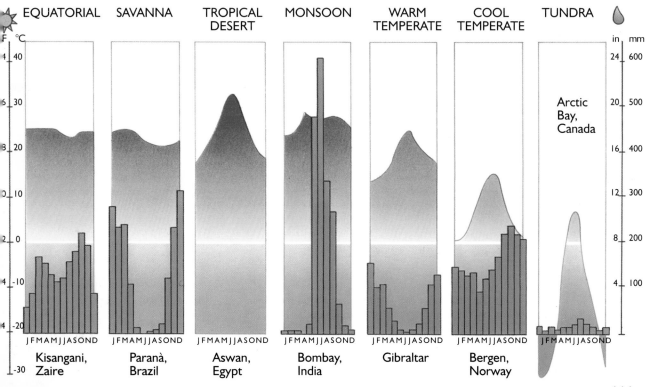

EQUATORIAL — Kisangani, Zaire
SAVANNA — Paranà, Brazil
TROPICAL DESERT — Aswan, Egypt
MONSOON — Bombay, India
WARM TEMPERATE — Gibraltar
COOL TEMPERATE — Bergen, Norway
TUNDRA — Arctic Bay, Canada

111

Nation facts

Nation	Area km² (sq miles)		Population	Main languages	Main religions	Currency
Afghanistan	652,225	(251,773)	16,600,000	Pushto/Dari	Islam	Afghani
Albania	28,748	(11,100)	3,300,000	Albanian	Islam/Orthodox	Lek
Algeria	2,381,741	(919,595)	26,000,000	Arabic/French/Berber	Islam	Dinar
Andorra	467	(180)	50,000	Catalan/French/Spanish	Roman Catholic	Franc/Pese
Angola	1,246,700	(481,354)	8,500,000	Portuguese	Roman Catholic/Animist	Kwanza
Antigua and Barbuda	442	(171)	100,000	English	Anglican	Dollar
Argentina	2,766,889	(1,068,302)	32,700,000	Spanish	Roman Catholic	Austral
Australia	7,682,300	(2,966,150)	17,500,000	English	Anglican/Roman Catholic	Dollar
Austria	83,855	(32,367)	7,700,000	German	Roman Catholic	Schilling
Bahamas	13,939	(5,382)	300,000	English	Baptist/Anglican/Roman Catholic	Dollar
Bahrain	691	(267)	500,000	Arabic	Islam	Dinar
Bangladesh	143,998	(55,598)	116,600,000	Bengali	Islam	Taka
Barbados	430	(166)	300,000	English	Anglican	Dollar
Belgium	30,519	(11,783)	9,900,000	Flemish/French	Roman Catholic	Franc
Belize	22,965	(8,867)	200,000	English/Creole/Spanish	Roman Catholic	Dollar
Benin	112,622	(43,484)	4,800,000	French/Fon	Aminist/Islam	Franc
Bhutan	46,500	(17,954)	700,000	Dzongkha	Buddhism	Ngultrum
Bolivia	1,098,581	(424,164)	7,500,000	Spanish/Quéchua	Roman Catholic	Boliviano
Bosnia-Herzegovina	51,113	(19,735)	4,360,000	Serbo-Croat	Orthodox/Islam	Dinar
Botswana	582,000	(224,711)	1,300,000	English/Setswana	Animist/Anglican	Pula
Brazil	8,511,965	(3,286,488)	153,300,000	Portuguese	Roman Catholic	Cruzeiro
Brunei	5,765	(2,226)	300,000	Malay/Chinese/English	Islam	Dollar
Bulgaria	110,912	(42,823)	9,000,000	Bulgarian	Orthodox	Lev
Burkina Faso	274,200	(105,869)	9,400,000	French/Mossi	Animist/Islam	Franc
Burundi	27,834	(10,747)	5,800,000	Kirundi/French/Kiswahili	Roman Catholic	Franc
Cambodia	181,035	(69,898)	7,100,000	Khmer/French	Buddhism	Riel
Cameroon	475,442	(183,569)	11,400,000	French/English	Animist/Islam/Roman Catholic	Franc
Canada	9,970,610	(3,849,674)	26,800,000	English/French	Roman Catholic	Dollar
Cape Verde	4,033	(1,557)	400,000	Portuguese/Crioulu	Roman Catholic	Escudo
Central African Republic	622,984	(240,535)	3,000,000	French/Sangho	Animist/Roman Catholic	Franc
Chad	1,284,000	(495,790)	5,100,000	French/Arabic	Islam/Animist	Franc
Chile	756,945	(292,258)	13,400,000	Spanish	Roman Catholic	Peso
China	9,571,300	(3,695,500)	1,151,300,000	Chinese	Buddhism/Islam/Confucianism	Yuan
Colombia	1,141,748	(40,831)	33,600,000	Spanish	Roman Catholic	Peso
Comoros	1,862	(719)	500,000	French/Arabic	Islam	Franc
Commonwealth of Independent States	21,500,581	(8,301,415)	223,220,000	Russian/Ukranian/Belorussian	Russian Orthodox/Islam	Rouble
Congo	342,000	(132,047)	2,300,000	French/Lingala	Roman Catholic	Franc
Costa Rica	51,100	(19,730)	3,100,000	Spanish	Roman Catholic	Colón
Croatia	56,526	(21,825)	4,660,000	Serbo-Croat	Roman Catholic	Dinar
Cuba	110,860	(42,803)	10,700,000	Spanish	Roman Catholic	Peso
Cyprus	9,251	(3,572)	700,000	Greek/Turkish	Orthodox/Islam	Pound
Czechlands	78,864	(30,449)	10,400,000	Czech	Roman Catholic/Protestant	Koruna
Denmark	43,092	(16,638)	5,100,000	Danish	Lutheran	Krone
Djibouti	23,200	(8,950)	400,000	Arabic/French	Islam	Franc
Dominica	751	(290)	100,000	English/French patois	Roman Catholic	Dollar
Dominican Republic	48,422	(18,696)	7,300,000	Spanish	Roman Catholic	Peso

Nation	Area km² (sq miles)		Population	Main languages	Main religions	Currency
Ecuador	270,670	(104,506)	10,800,000	Spanish	Roman Catholic	Sucre
Egypt	997,739	(385,229)	54,500,000	Arabic	Islam	Pound
El Salvador	21,393	(8,260)	5,400,000	Spanish	Roman Catholic	Colón
Equatorial Guinea	28,051	(10,831)	400,000	Spanish/Fang/Bubi	Roman Catholic	Franc
Estonia	45,091	(17,410)	1,573,000	Estonian	Lutheran	Kroon
Ethiopia	1,223,600	(472,435)	53,200,000	Amharic/Arabic	Islam/Ethiopian Orthodox	Birr
Fiji	18,376	(7,095)	700,000	English/Fijian/Hindi	Methodist/Hindu	Dollar
Finland	338,145	(130,557)	5,000,000	Finnish	Lutheran	Markka
France	543,965	(210,026)	56,700,000	French	Roman Catholic	Franc
Gabon	267,667	(103,347)	1,200,000	French	Animist/Roman Catholic	Franc
Gambia	11,295	(4,361)	900,000	English	Islam	Dalasi
Germany	357,050	(137,857)	79,500,000	German	Lutheran	Deutschmark
Georgia	2,716,588	(1,048,880)	5,500,000	Georgian	Georgian Church	Rouble
Ghana	238,537	(92,099)	15,500,000	English/Asante/Ewe	Animist/Protestant	Cedi
Greece	131,957	(50,949)	10,100,000	Greek	Orthodox	Drachma
Grenada	344	(133)	100,000	English	Roman Catholic/Anglican	Dollar
Guatemala	108,889	(42,042)	9,500,000	Spanish	Roman Catholic	Quetzal
Guinea	245,857	(94,926)	7,500,000	French/Soussou/Manika	Islam	Franc
Guinea-Bissau	36,125	(13,948)	100,000,000	Portuguese/Crioulo	Animist/Islam	Peso
Guyana	214,969	(83,000)	800,000	English/Hindi/Urdu	Hindu	Dollar
Haiti	27,750	(10,714)	6,300,000	Creole/French	Voodoo/Roman Catholic	Gourde
Honduras	112,088	(43,277)	5,300,000	Spanish	Roman Catholic	Lempira
Hungary	93,036	(35,921)	10,400,000	Magyar	Roman Catholic	Forint
Iceland	103,001	(39,769)	300,000	Icelandic	Lutheran	Króna
India	3,287,263	(1,269,212)	859,200,000	Hindi/English	Hindu/Islam	Rupee
Indonesia	1,919,443	(741,101)	181,400,000	Bahasa Indonesia	Islam	Rupiah
Iran	1,648,000	(636,296)	58,600,000	Farsi/Azerbaijani	Islam	Rial
Iraq	441,839	(170,595)	17,100,000	Arabic/Kurdish	Islam	Dinar
Ireland	70,282	(27,136)	3,500,000	Irish/English	Roman Catholic	Pound
Israel	21,946	(8,473)	6,600,000	Hebrew/Arabic	Judaism/Islam	Shekel
Italy	301,277	(116,324)	57,700,000	Italian	Roman Catholic	Lira
Ivory Coast	322,462	(124,503)	12,500,000	French/Dioula/Baoulé	Animist/Islam/Roman Catholic	Franc
Jamaica	10,991	(4,244)	2,500,000	English	Protestant	Dollar
Japan	377,815	(145,874)	123,800,000	Japanese	Shintoism/Buddhism	Yen
Jordan	89,206	(34,443)	3,400,000	Arabic	Islam	Dinar
Kenya	580,367	(224,081)	25,200,000	Swahili/English	Animist/Roman Catholic	Shilling
Kiribati	717	(277)	69,600	English/I-Kiribati	Roman Catholic/Protestant	Dollar
Korea, North	120,538	(46,540)	21,800,000	Korean	Buddhism/Confucianism/Daoism	Won
Korea, South	99,143	(38,279)	43,200,000	Korean	Buddhism/Christianity	Won
Kuwait	17,818	(6,880)	1,400,000	Arabic	Islam	Dinar
Laos	236,800	(91,400)	4,100,000	Lao	Buddhism	Kip
Latvia	63,687	(24,590)	2,681,000	Latvian	Lutheran/Roman Catholic	Rouble
Lebanon	10,452	(4,036)	3,400,000	Arabic	Islam/Christianity	Pound
Lesotho	30,355	(11,720)	1,800,000	Sesotho/English	Roman Catholic	Loti
Liberia	111,369	(43,000)	2,700,000	English	Animist	Dollar
Libya	1,759,540	(679,363)	4,400,000	Arabic	Islam	Dinar
Liechtenstein	160	(62)	30,000	German	Roman Catholic	Franc
Lithuania	65,177	(25,165)	3,690,000	Lithuanian	Roman Catholic	Rouble

Nation	Area km² (sq miles)		Population	Main languages	Main religions	Currency
Luxembourg	2,586	(999)	400,000	Letzeburgish/French	Roman Catholic	Franc
Madagascar	587,041	(226,658)	12,400,000	Malagasy/French	Animist/Christianity	Franc
Malawi	118,484	(45,747)	9,400,000	English/Chichewa	Animist/Roman Catholic	Kwacha
Malaysia	329,758	(127,320)	18,300,000	Bahasa Malaysia/English/ Chinese	Islam	Dollar
Maldives	298	(115)	200,000	Dhivehi	Islam	Rufiyaa
Mali	1,240,192	(478,841)	8,300,000	French/Bambara	Islam/Animist	Franc
Malta	316	(122)	400,000	Maltese/English	Roman Catholic	Lira
Mauritania	1,030,700	(397,950)	2,100,000	Arabic/French	Islam	Ouguiya
Mauritius	2,040	(788)	1,100,000	English/Creole/Hindi	Hindu/Roman Catholic/Islam	Rupee
Mexico	1,958,201	(756,066)	85,700,000	Spanish	Roman Catholic	Peso
Monaco	2.21	(0.85)	29,000	French/Monegasque	Roman Catholic	Franc
Mongolia	1,565,000	(604,250)	2,200,000	Khalkh Mongolian/Kazakh	Officially no religion	Tugrik
Morocco	710,850	(274,461)	26,400,000	Arabic/Berber/French	Islam	Dirham
Mozambique	799,380	(308,641)	16,100,000	Portuguese	Animist	Metical
Myanmar (Burma)	676,552	(261,218)	42,100,000	Burmese	Buddhism	Kyat
Namibia	823,168	(317,827)	1,500,000	Afrikaans/English	Lutheran/Roman Catholic	Rand
Nauru	21	(8)	8,100	Nauruan/English	Protestant/Roman Catholic	Dollar
Nepal	147,181	(56,827)	19,600,000	Nepali/Maithir	Hindu/Buddhism	Rupee
Netherlands	41,785	(33,937)	15,000,000	Dutch	Roman Catholic/Protestant	Guilder
New Zealand	269,057	(103,883)	3,500,000	English/Maori	Protestant/Roman Catholic	Dollar
Nicaragua	120,254	(46,430)	3,900,000	Spanish/Miskito	Roman Catholic	Córdoba
Niger	1,267,000	(489,191)	8,000,000	French/Hausa	Islam	Franc
Nigeria	923,768	(356,669)	122,500,000	English	Islam/Christianity	Naira
Norway	323,878	(125,050)	4,300,000	Norwegian	Lutheran	Krone
Oman	300,000	(120,000)	1,600,000	Arabic/Baluchi	Islam	Rial
Pakistan	803,943	(310,403)	117,500,000	Urdu/Punjabi/Sindhi	Islam	Rupee
Panama	77,082	(29,762)	2,500,000	Spanish	Roman Catholic	Balboa
Papua New Guinea	462,840	(178,704)	3,900,000	English/Pidgin English	Roman Catholic/Protestant	Kina
Paraguay	406,752	(157,048)	4,400,000	Spanish/Guaraní	Roman Catholic	Guaraní
Peru	1,258,216	(496,225)	22,000,000	Spanish/Quechua/Aymara	Roman Catholic	Inti
Philippines	300,000	(120,000)	62,300,000	Philipino/Tagalog/English Spanish/Cebuano	Roman Catholic	Peso
Poland	312,683	(120,727)	38,200,000	Polish	Roman Catholic	Zloty
Portugal	92,072	(33,549)	10,400,000	Portuguese	Roman Catholic	Esucdo
Qatar	11,437	(4,416)	500,000	Arabic	Islam	Riyal
Romania	237,500	(91,699)	23,400,000	Romanian	Orthodox	Leu
Rwanda	26,338	(10,169)	7,500,000	French/Kinyarwanda	Animist/Roman Catholic	Franc
St Christopher and Nevis	262	(101)	40,000	English	Anglican	Dollar
St Lucia	616	(238)	200,000	English/French patois	Roman Catholic	Dollar
St Vincent and the Grenadines	389	(150)	100,000	English	Anglican/Methodist/Roman Catholic	Dollar
San Marino	61	(23)	23,000	Italian	Roman Catholic	Lira
São Tomé and Príncipe	964	(372)	100,000	Portuguese	Roman Catholic	Dobra
Saudi Arabia	2,240,000	(864,869)	15,500,000	Arabic	Islam	Riyal
Senegal	196,722	(75,954)	7,500,000	French	Islam	Franc
Seychelles	454	(173)	100,000	Creole/English/French	Roman Catholic	Rupee
Sierra Leone	71,740	(27,699)	4,300,000	English/Krio/Mende	Animist	Leone

Nation	Area km² (sq miles)		Population	Main languages	Main religions	Currency
Singapore	623	(240)	2,800,000	Malay/Chinese/English/Tamil	Buddhism	Dollar
Slovakia	49,035	(18,932)	5,400,000	Slovak	Roman Catholic/Protestant	Koruna
Slovenia	20,240	(7,815)	1,930,000	Slovene	Roman Catholic	Dinar
Solomon Islands	27,556	(10,639)	300,000	English/Pidgin English	Protestant/Roman Catholic	Dollar
Somalia	637,657	(246,201)	7,700,000	Somali/Arabic	Islam	Shilling
South Africa	2,347,661	(906,437)	40,600,000	English/Afrikaans/Xhosa/Zulu/Sesotho	Christianity/Hindu/Islam	Rand
Spain	504,782	(194,897)	39,000,000	Spanish/Catalan	Roman Catholic	Peseta
Sri Lanka	65,610	(25,332)	17,400,000	Sinhala/Tamil/English	Buddhism/Hindu	Rupee
Sudan	2,505,813	(967,500)	25,900,000	Arabic	Islam	Pound
Surinam	163,265	(63,037)	400,000	Dutch/Sranang Togo/Hindi/Javanese	Hindu/Roman Catholic/Islam/Moravian	Guilder
Swaziland	17,363	(6,704)	800,000	SiSwati/English	Christianity	Lilangeni
Sweden	449,964	(173,732)	8,600,000	Swedish	Lutheran	Krona
Switzerland	41,293	(15,943)	6,800,000	German/French/Italian/Romansch	Roman Catholic/Protestant	Franc
Syria	185,180	(71,498)	12,800,000	Arabic	Islam	Pound
Taiwan	38,981	(13,893)	20,500,000	Chinese	Buddhism/Daoism	Dollar
Tanzania	945,087	(364,900)	26,900,000	English/Swahili	Islam/Roman Catholic	Shiling
Thailand	513,115	(198,115)	58,800,000	Thai	Buddhism/Islam	Baht
Togo	56,785	(21,925)	3,800,000	French/Ewe/Kabiye	Animist/Roman Catholic/Islam	Franc
Tonga	748	(289)	95,900	Tongan/English	Methodist/Roman Catholic	Dollar
Trinidad and Tobago	5,130	(1,981)	1,300,000	English/Hindi	Roman Catholic/Hindu/Anglican	Dollar
Tunisia	163,610	(63,170)	8,400,000	Arabic	Islam	Dinar
Turkey	779,452	(300,948)	58,500,000	Turkish	Islam	Lira
Tuvalu	26	(10)	9,000	Tuvaluan/English	Protestant	Dollar
Uganda	241,139	(93,104)	18,700,000	English/Swahili	Roman Catholic/Protestant/Animist	Shiling
United Arab Emirates	77,700	(30,000)	2,400,000	Arabic/English	Islam	Dirham
United Kingdom	244,103	(94,249)	57,500,000	English	Anglican/Roman Catholic	Pound
United States of America	9,372,614	(3,618,770)	252,800,000	English	Roman Catholic/Baptist	Dollar
Uruguay	176,215	(68,037)	3,100,000	Spanish	Roman Catholic	Peso
Vanuatu	12,189	(4,706)	200,000	English/French	Protestant	Vatu
Vatican City	0.44	(0.17)	850	Italian/Latin	Roman Catholic	Lira
Venezuela	912,050	(352,144)	20,100,000	Spanish	Roman Catholic	Bolívar
Vietnam	329,566	(127,246)	67,600,000	Vietnamese	Buddhism	Dông
Western Samoa	2,831	(1,093)	200,000	English/Samoan	Protestant	Tala
Yemen	531,869	(205,356)	10,100,000	Arabic	Islam	Riyal
Yugoslavia	127,841	(49,360)	12,320,000	Serbo-Croat	Orthodox/Roman Catholic	Dinar
Zaire	2,344,885	(905,365)	37,800,000	French	Roman Catholic	Zaïre
Zambia	752,614	(290,586)	8,400,000	English	Christianity/Animist	Kwacha
Zimbabwe	390,759	(150,873)	10,000,000	English/Chishona/Sindebele	Anglican/Roman Catholic	Dollar

Glossary

Words that are explained in this glossary are printed in **bold type**.

Alternative energy. Energy from natural sources, such as the wind and the Sun.

Antarctic Circle. An imaginary line 66½° south of the **Equator**, bordering the sea and frozen land around the **South Pole**.

Arctic Circle. An imaginary line 66½° north of the **Equator**, bordering the area of frozen sea and land around the **North Pole**.

Atmosphere. The gases which surround the Earth.

Atmospheric pressure. The weight of the **atmosphere** pressing down on the Earth's surface.

Boreal forests. Forests of **conifers** which grow in the northern **hemisphere**.

Cardinal points. The eight main directions on a compass: north, north-east, east, south-east, south, south-west, west, and north-west.

Cartography. The practice of mapmaking.

CFCs (Chlorofluorocarbons). Gases made by the chemical industry for use in refrigerators, aerosols and packaging material. They attack the **ozone layer**.

Climate. The variations in weather pattern, including temperature, rainfall and wind, of a particular area, measured over many years.

Condensation. The changing of a gas into a liquid as it cools down, for example when water vapour changes to water.

Conifer. An evergreen tree with needle-like leaves which does not lose its leaves in winter.

Conservation. Protecting the **environment** around us and the animals and plants which live in it.

Continent. One of the Earth's six main land masses, which are Africa, America, Antarctica, Asia, Australia and Europe.

Continental drift. The slow movement of the **plates** which make up the Earth's **crust**.

Contours. Lines drawn on maps which join places that are the same height above sea-level.

Conurbation. An area where several large towns or cities have merged together to make one big city.

Core. The middle of the Earth, which is made up of a solid metal centre, called the inner core, and a hot, liquid metal outer core.

Crust. The solid outer layer of the Earth, which makes up the Earth's land surface.

Deciduous tree. A broad-leaved tree which loses its leaves in winter.

Demography. The study of population and how it changes.

Depression. An area of low **atmospheric pressure**, where an area of warm air is surrounded by cooler air.

Desert. An area of land that has little or no rain and where only a few plants and animals live.

Development. The improvement of a country's industry, wealth and standard of living.

Environment. The natural world around us and the features of our surroundings that have been built and changed by people.

Equator. The imaginary line around the middle of the Earth, at latitude 0°.

Equatorial. Anything relating to the **Equator**.

Erosion. Wearing away of the Earth's surface or buildings by wind, water, or ice, for example.

Evaporation. The changing of a liquid into gas when it warms up, for example when water turns into water vapour.

Fault. A weak line in the Earth's **crust**, which causes breaks in the surface.

Fossil fuels. Coal, oil and natural gas, which were made by **fossilization**, and which can be burned to produce energy.

Fossilization. The way in which the hard parts of animals and plants are preserved within layers of **rock** over millions of years.

Front. A narrow layer of air between two large masses of air that are different in temperature and **humidity**.

Fuel. A material which can be used to produce heat.

Geology. The study of **rocks** and **minerals**.

Gravity. The force that attracts objects toward each other. Gravity attracts everything on and around the Earth to its centre.

Greenhouse Effect. The ability of the Earth's **atmosphere** to keep heat in, which many scientists say is becoming greater.

Heavy industry. The type of industry that needs large machines and uses heavy **raw materials**, such as steel-making.

Hemisphere. One half of the globe, either side of the **Equator** or either side of the **Prime Meridian**, for example.

Humidity. The amount of water vapour (water in the form of a gas) in the **atmosphere**.

Indian subcontinent. The area covered by India, Pakistan, Bangladesh, Nepal, Bhutan and Sri Lanka.

Industrial Revolution. A period of change when a country's industry and transport improve greatly, the population expands, and towns and cities grow quickly. The first Industrial Revolution was in Britain, between 1750 and 1850.

Irrigation. How farmers bring water to their plants, along channels or by using machines.

Latitude. Distance north or south of the **Equator**, measured in degrees.

Light industry. The type of industry that uses few **raw materials** and produces light, easily transportable goods.

Longitude. Distance east or west of the **Prime Meridian**, measured in degrees.

Magma. Hot, molten rock beneath the Earth's **crust**.

Meteorology. The study of weather and **climate** patterns.

Mineral. A natural substance that is not an animal or a plant.

Non-renewable resource. A **resource** that cannot be reused, or that is being used up faster than it is being reproduced, such as coal.

North Pole. One end of the Earth's axis, at **latitude** 90°N.

Ocean. One of the four large masses of salt-water which cover the Earth's surface: the Arctic, the Atlantic, the Indian and the Pacific Oceans.

Ore. A **rock** which contains metal.

Ozone layer. A layer of the Earth's **atmosphere** that contains the gas ozone, which is a form of oxygen. The ozone layer filters out the Sun's harmful rays.

Plates. The separate pieces of the Earth's **crust**.

Polar. Anything relating to the area around either the **North** or the **South Pole**.

Pollute. To make something dirty or unpleasant, especially the **environment**.

Precipitation. Water that falls from the **atmosphere** to the Earth's surface, in the form of rain, snow, sleet or hail.

Prime Meridian. An imaginary line from the **North Pole** to the **South Pole**, following the 0° line of **longitude**.

Rainforest. Evergreen, deciduous forest that grows in the **Tropics**.

Raw materials. Basic natural materials, such as wood, crops or oil, which are used in manufacturing.

Renewable resource. A **resource** that can be reused over and over again, such as water or wind.

Resource. Anything in the world that can be used by people.

Rock. A natural substance which is made up of one or more **minerals**.

Rural. Anything relating to the countryside, rather than the city.

Satellite. Something that travels around a central object, for example the Moon, which travels around the Earth.

Sea. An area of **ocean**, usually enclosed by or near to land, for example the Mediterranean Sea.

Sediment. Particles of **rock**, plant or animal matter that have been washed or blown from the landscape.

South Pole. One end of the Earth's axis, at **latitude** 90°S.

Spring. A place where water naturally comes out of the ground.

Stalactite. An icicle-shaped mass of **minerals** which hangs from a cave roof, formed by water evaporating as it drips through limestone. A **stalagmite** is the same, except it sits on the floor and points up to the ceiling.

Suburb. An area of usually newer buildings surrounding a town or city.

Temperate forests. Forests made up of **conifers** and **deciduous trees**, which grow between the **polar** areas and the tropical areas.

Tropics. The area between the Tropic of Cancer and the Tropic of Capricorn. These are imaginary lines which circle the globe. The Tropic of Cancer is $23\frac{1}{2}°$ north of the **Equator** and the Tropic of Capricorn is $23\frac{1}{2}°$ south of the **Equator**.

Tundra. Frozen land, bordering the Arctic, where no trees grow.

Urban. Anything relating to towns or cities, rather than countryside.

Water cycle. The circular journey of the Earth's water from the **sea** to the air to the land and back again.

Map index

This index helps you to find places on the maps. For each place name, it gives the page number of the map, the grid reference and the latitude and longitude. You can find out about latitude and longitude and how to read grid references on pages 8-13.

Some abbreviations have been used in the index to show what each entry refers to. These are as follows:

mt.	mountain	mts.	mountains
r.	river	st.	state or province
i.	island	is.	islands

A

Abadan Iran **104 B2** 30°21'N 48°15'E
Abéché Chad **98 E3** 13°49'N 20°49'E
Abidjan Ivory Coast **98 B4** 5°19'N 4°01'W
Abu Dhabi United Arab Emirates **104 C3** 24°27'N 54°23'E
Abuja Nigeria **98 C4** 9°12'N 7°11'E
Acapulco Mexico **96 B3** 16°51'N 99°56'W
Accra Ghana **98 B4** 5°33'N 0°15'W
Aconcagua mt. Argentina **97 F8** 32°39'S 70°00'W
Adamawa Highlands mts. Cameroon/Nigeria **98 D4** 7°05'N 12°00'E
Addis Ababa Ethiopia **98 F4** 9°03'N 38°42'N
Adelaide Australia **106 B4** 34°56'S 138°36'E
Aden, Gulf of Indian Ocean **104 B4-C4**
Adriatic Sea Europe **100-101 E7**
Aegean Sea Europe **101 F8**
Afghanistan Asia **104 D2**
Agadès Niger **98 C3** 17°00'N 7°56'E
Agadir Morocco **98 B1** 30°26'N 9°36'W
Ahmadabad India **104 E3** 23°02'N 72°37'E
Ajaccio France **100 D7** 41°55'N 8°44'E
Aktyubinsk Kazakhstan **102 E3** 50°16'N 57°13'E
Alabama st. USA **95 J5**
Aland Is. Finland **101 E3**
Alaska st. USA **94 C2**
Alaska, Gulf of USA **94 D3**
Albania Europe **101 F7**
Albany Australia **106 A4** 34°57'S 117°54'E
Albert, Lake Uganda/Zaire **99 F4** 1°45'N 31°00'E
Alberta st. Canada **94 G3**
Ålborg Denmark **100 D4** 57°03'N 9°56'E
Aldan Russian Federation **103 L3** 58°44'N 125°22'E
Aleutian Is. Alaska **94 B3**
Alexander Bay South Africa **99 D7** 28°36'S 16°26'E
Alexandria Egypt **98 E1** 31°13'N 29°55'E
Algeria Africa **98 B2-C2**
Algiers Algeria **98 C1** 36°50'N 3°00'E
Alice Springs Australia **98 B4** 23°42'S 133°52'E
Al Jawf Libya **98 E2** 24°12'N 28°18'E
Alma-Ata Kazakhstan **102 G4** 43°19'N 76°55'E
Al Manamah Bahrain **104 C3** 26°12'N 50°36'E
Almeria Spain **100 C8** 36°50'N 2°27'W
Amazon r. Brazil **96 F5**
Amderma Russian Federation **102 F2** 69°44'N 61°35'E
American Samoa is. Pacific Ocean **107 E3**
Amman Jordan **104 A2** 31°57'N 35°56'E
Amsterdam Netherlands **100 D5** 52°22'N 4°54'E
Amu Darya r. Uzbekistan **102 F5**
Amundsen Sea Antarctica **109**
Amur r. Asia **103 L3-M3**
Anadyr Russian Federation **103 Q2** 64°40'N 177°32'E
Anadyr r. Russian Federation **103 Q2**
Anchorage Alaska **94 D2** 61°10'N 150°00'W
Andaman and Nicobar Is. Indian Ocean **105 G4-G5**
Andes mts. Peru/Chile **97 E6-E7**
Andorra Europe **100 D7**
Angara r. Russian Federation **102 I3**
Angola Africa **99 D6**
Ankara Turkey **100 G8** 39°55'N 32°50'E
Annaba Algeria **98 C1** 36°55'N 7°47'E
Antalya Turkey **101 G8** 36°53'N 30°42'E
Antananarivo Madagascar **99 G6** 18°55'S 47°31'E
Antarctic Circle 109
Antarctic Peninsula Antarctica **109**
Antigua and Barbuda Central America **96 F3**

Apia Western Samoa **107 E3** 13°48'S 171°45'W
Appenines mts. Italy **100 E7**
Arabian Sea Asia **104 D3-D4**
Arafura Sea Australasia **106 B3**
Aral Sea Kazakhstan **102 F4**
Arapiraca Brazil **97 I5** 9°45'S 36°40'W
Ararat, Mt. Turkey **101 H8** 39°45'N 44°15'E
Archipelago Pacific Ocean **107 G3-G4**
Arctic Bay North West Territories Canada **95 J1** 73°05'N 85°20'W
Arctic Circle 108
Arctic Ocean 93 N1
Arequipa Peru **97 E6** 16°25'S 71°32'W
Argentina South America **97 F7**
Arica Chile **97 E6** 18°29'S 70°20'W
Arkansas st. USA **95 I5**
Arkhangel'sk Russian Federation **102 D2** 64°32'N 41°10'E
Arizona st. USA **94 G5**
Armenia Asia **102 D4**
Ashkhabad Turkmenistan **102 E5** 37°58'N 58°24'E
Asmera Ethiopia **99 F3** 15°20'N 38°58'E
Astrakhan Russian Federation **102 D4** 46°22'N 48°00'E
Asunción Paraguay **97 G7** 25°15'S 57°40'W
Aswan Egypt **98 F2** 24°05'N 32°56'E
Asyût Egypt **98 F2** 27°14'N 31°07'E
Atacama Desert South America **97 F6-F7**
Atbara Sudan **99 F3** 17°42'N 33°59'E
Athabasca, Lake Alberta Canada **94 H3** 59°07'N 110°00'W
Athens Greece **101 F8** 38°00'N 23°44'E
Atlanta Georgia USA **95 J5** 33°45'N 84°23'W
Atlantic Ocean 92 I5-J5
Atlas Mts. Morocco **98 B1**
Auckland New Zealand **107 D4** 36°55'S 174°45'E
Auckland Is. Pacific Ocean **107 D5**
Australia 106 B4
Australian Antarctic Territory Antarctica **109**
Austria Europe **100-101 E6**
Ayers Rock Australia mt. **106 B4** 25°18'S 131°18'E
Azerbaijan Asia **102 D4**
Azov, Sea of Ukraine/Russian Federation **102 C4**

B

Baffin Bay Greenland/Canada **95 M1**
Baffin I. North West Territories Canada **95 K1** 68°50'N 70°00'W
Baghdad Iraq **104 B2** 33°20'N 44°26'E
Bahamas Central America **96 E2**
Bahía Blanca Argentina **97 F8** 38°45'S 62°15'W
Bahrain Asia **104 C3**
Baikal Lake Russian Federation **103 K3**
Baku Azerbaijan **102 E4** 40°22'N 49°53'E
Balearic Is. Spain **100 D8**
Bali i. Indonesia **105 I6** 8°20'S 115°07'E
Balikpapan Indonesia **105 I6** 1°15'S 116°50'E
Balkan Mts. Bulgaria **101 F7**
Balkhash, Lake Kazakhstan **102 G4**
Balleny Is. Antarctica **109**
Baltic Sea Europe **101 E4**
Bamako Mali **98 B3** 12°40'N 7°59'W
Bandar Seri Begawan Brunei **105 I5** 4°56'N 114°58'E
Bangalore India **104 E4** 12°58'N 77°35'E
Bangassou Central African Republic **98 E4** 4°50'N 23°07'E
Bangkok Thailand **105 H4** 13°44'N 100°30'E
Bangladesh Asia **105 G3**
Bangui Central African Republic **98 D4** 4°23'N 18°37'E
Banjul The Gambia **98 A3** 13°28'N 16°39'W
Banks I. North West Territories Canada **94 F1** 73°00'N 122°00'W
Barbados Central America **96 G3**
Barcelona Spain **100 D7** 41°23'N 2°11'E
Barents Sea Arctic Ocean **93 O1-O2**
Barnaul Russian Federation **102 H3** 53°21'N 83°15'E
Barranquilla Colombia **96 E3** 11°10'N 74°50'W
Basel Switzerland **100 D6** 47°33'N 7°35'E
Bass Strait Australia **106 C4**
Batna Algeria **98 C1** 33°35'N 6°11'E
Beaufort Sea Arctic Ocean **108**
Béchar Algeria **98 B1** 31°37'N 2°13'W
Beijing China **105 I1** 39°55'N 116°25'E
Béira Mozambique **99 F6** 19°49'S 34°52'E
Beirut Lebanon **104 A2** 33°52'N 35°30'E
Belem Brazil **96 H5** 1°27'S 48°29'W
Belfast UK **100 C5** 54°36'N 5°57'W

Belgium Europe **100 D5**
Belgorod Russian Federation **102 C3** 50°38'N 36°36'E
Belgrade Yugoslavia **101 F7** 44°49'N 20°28'E
Belize Central America **96 D3**
Belmopan Belize **96 D3** 17°25'N 88°46'W
Belo Horizonte Brazil **97 H6** 19°45'S 43°54'W
Belorussia Europe **102 B3**
Bengal, Bay of Indian Ocean **105 F4-G4**
Benghazi Libya **98 E1** 32°07'N 20°05'E
Benin Africa **98 C3-C4**
Benue r. Nigeria **98 C4**
Bergen Norway **100 D3** 60°23'N 5°20'E
Bering Sea 92 A3
Bering Strait Arctic Ocean **94 B2**
Berkner I. Antarctica **109** 79°30'S 50°00'W
Berlin Germany **100 E5** 52°31'N 13°24'E
Bern Switzerland **100 D6** 46°57'N 7°26'E
Betroka Madagascar **99 G7** 23°16'S 46°06'E
Beyla Guinea **98 B4** 8°42'N 8°39'W
Bhopal India **105 E3** 23°16'N 77°24'E
Bhutan Asia **105 F3-G3**
Billings Montana USA **94 H4** 45°47'N 108°27'W
Birmingham UK **100 C5** 52°30'N 1°55'W
Birmingham Alabama USA **95 J5** 33°30'N 86°55'W
Biscay, Bay of France **100 C6**
Bishkek Kyrgyzstan **102 G4** 42°53'N 74°46'E
Bissau Guinea-Bissau **98 A3** 11°52'N 15°39'W
Black Sea Europe **101 G7**
Blagoveshchensk Russian Federation **103 L3** 50°19'N 127°30'E
Blanc, Mont mt. France **100 D6** 45°50'N 6°52'E
Blantyre Malawi **99 F6** 15°46'S 35°00'E
Bloemfontein South Africa **99 E7** 29°07'S 26°14'E
Blue Nile r. Sudan **98 F3**
Bobo Dioulasso Burkina Faso **98 B3** 11°11'N 4°18'W
Bogotá Colombia **96 E4** 4°38'N 74°05'W
Boise Idaho USA **94 G4** 43°37'N 116°13'W
Bolivia South America **97 F6**
Bombay India **104 E4** 18°58'N 72°50'E
Bonn Germany **100 D5** 50°44'N 7°05'E
Bordeaux France **100 C7** 44°50'N 0°34'W
Borneo i. Asia **105 I6** 1°00'N 114°00'E
Bornholm i. Denmark **101 E4** 55°10'N 15°00'E
Bosnia-Herzegovina Europe **101 E7**
Boston Massachusetts USA **95 K4** 42°21'N 71°04'W
Bothnia, Gulf of Europe **101 E3**
Botswana Africa **99 E7**
Bougainville I. Pacific Ocean **107 C3** 6°00'S 155°00'E
Brahmaputra r. Asia **105 G3**
Brásília Brazil **97 H6** 15°45'W 47°57'W
Bratislava Slovakia **101 E6** 48°10'N 17°10'E
Bratsk Russian Federation **103 J3** 56°20'N 101°15'E
Brazil South America **97 G5**
Brazzaville Congo **99 D5** 4°14'S 15°10'E
Bremen Germany **100 D5** 53°05'N 8°49'E
Brest France **100 C6** 48°24'N 4°29'W
Brisbane Australia **106 C4** 27°30'S 153°00'E
British Antarctic Territory Antarctica **109**
British Columbia st. Canada **94 F3**
Brno Czechlands **101 E6** 49°11'N 16°39'E
Brownsville Texas USA **95 I6** 25°54'N 97°30'W
Brunei Asia **105 I5**
Brussels Belgium **100 D5** 50°50'N 4°23'E
Bryansk Russian Federation **102 C3** 53°15'N 34°09'E
Bucharest Romania **101 F7** 44°25'N 26°06'E
Budapest Hungary **101 E6** 47°30'N 19°03'E
Buenos Aires Argentina **97 G8** 34°40'S 58°25'W
Bujumbura Burundi **99 E5** 3°22'S 29°21'E
Bulawayo Zimbabwe **99 E7** 20°10'S 28°43'E
Bulgaria Europe **101 F7**
Burkina Faso Africa **98 B3**
Burma see Myanmar
Burundi Africa **99 F5**
Buta Zaire **99 E4** 2°50'N 24°50'E

C

Cabinda Angola **99 D5** 5°34'S 12°12'E
Cádiz Spain **100 C8** 36°32'N 6°18'W
Cágliari Italy **100 D8** 39°13'N 9°06'E
Cairns Australia **106 C3** 16°51'S 145°43'E
Cairo Egypt **98 F2** 30°03'N 31°15'E
Calabar Nigeria **98 C4** 4°56'N 8°22'E
Calcutta India **105 F3** 22°32'N 88°22'E
Calgary Alberta Canada **94 G3** 51°00'N 114°10'W
Cali Colombia **96 E4** 3°24'N 76°30'W
California st. USA **94 G5**

California, Gulf of Mexico **96 A2**
Callao Peru **97 E6** 12°05'S 77°08'W
Cambodia Asia **105 H4**
Cameroon Africa **98 D4**
Campeche Mexico **96 C3** 19°50'N 90°30'W
Campinas Brazil **97 H7** 22°54'S 47°06'W
Campo Grande Brazil **97 G7** 20°24'S 54°35'W
Canada North America **94-95**
Canary Is. Africa **98 A2**
Canberra Australia **106 C4** 35°18'S 149°08'E
Cantabrian Mts. Spain **100 C7**
Cape Town South Africa **99 D8** 33°55'S 18°27'E
Cape Verde Atlantic Ocean **92 K5**
Cape York Australia **106 C3** 12°40'S 142°20'E
Caracas Venezuela **96 F3** 10°35'N 66°56'W
Cardiff UK **100 C5** 51°28'N 3°11'W
Caribbean Sea Central America **96 E3-F3**
Carnarvon Australia **106 A4** 24°53'S 113°40'E
Caroline I. Kiribati **107 F3** 10°00'S 150°30'W
Caroline Is. Pacific Ocean **106 C2** 7°50'N 145°00'E
Carpathians mts. Europe **101 F6** 48°45'N 23°45'E
Casablanca Morocco **98 B1** 33°39'N 7°35'W
Caspian Sea Asia **102 E4**
Caucasus Mts. Russian Federation **102 D4**
Cebu Philippines **105 J4** 10°17'N 123°56'E
Celebes Sea Asia **105 J5**
Central African Republic Africa **98 D4-E4**
Central Siberian Plateau Russian Federation **103**
Ceuta Spain **100 C8** 35°53'N 5°19'W
Chad Africa **98 D3-E3**
Chad, Lake Chad **98 D3** 13°30'N 14°00'E
Changsha China **105 I3** 28°09'N 112°59'E
Channel Is. UK **100 C6** 49°28'N 2°13'W
Chari r. Chad **98 D3**
Charleston South Carolina USA **95 J5** 32°48'N 79°58'W
Charlotte North Carolina USA **95 J5** 35°03'N 80°50'W
Chelyabinsk Russian Federation **102 F3** 55°12'N 61°25'E
Chengdu China **105 H2** 30°41'N 104°05'E
Cherrapunji India **105 G3** 25°18'N 91°42'E
Cherskly Range mts. Russian Federation **103 N2**
Chesterfield Is. Pacific Ocean **107 C3**
Chicago Illinois USA **95 J4** 41°50'N 87°45'W
Chihuahua Mexico **96 B2** 28°38'N 106°05'W
Chile South America **97 E7-E8**
China Asia **105**
Chinde Mozambique **99 F6** 18°27'S 36°24'E
Chishinău Moldavia **102 B4** 47°00'N 28°50'E
Chita Russian Federation **103 K3** 52°03'N 113°35'E
Chittagong Bangladesh **105 G3** 22°20'N 91°50'E
Chongqing China **105 H3** 29°31'N 106°35'E
Christchurch New Zealand **107 D5** 43°33'S 172°40'E
Christmas I. Kiribati **107 E2** 1°52'N 157°20'W
Churchill r. Manitoba Canada **94 H3**
Ciudad Guayana Venezuela **96 F4** 8°22'N 62°40'W
Ciudad Juárez Mexico **96 B1** 31°44'N 106°29'W
Ciudad Madero Mexico **96 C2** 22°19'N 97°50'W
Ciudad Victoria Mexico **96 C2** 23°43'N 99°10'W
Clermont-Ferrand France **100 D6** 45°47'N 3°05'E
Cleveland Ohio USA **95 J4** 41°30'N 81°41'W
Cluj-Napoca Romania **101 F6** 46°47'N 23°37'E
Cochabamba Bolivia **97 F6** 17°24'S 66°09'W
Colombia South America **96 E4**
Colombo Sri Lanka **104 F5** 6°55'N 79°52'E
Colón Panama **96 D3** 9°21'N 79°54'W
Colorado r. USA **94 G5**
Colorado st. USA **94 H5**
Columbia r. Canada/USA **94 F4**
Communism Peak mt. Tajikistan **102 G5** 38°59'N 72°01'E
Comodoro Rivadavia Argentina **97 F9** 45°50'S 67°30'W
Comoros Africa **99 G6**
Conakry Guinea **98 A4** 9°30'N 13°43'W
Concepción Chile **97 E8** 36°50'S 73°03'W
Congo Africa **99 D5**
Cook, Mt. New Zealand **107 D5** 43°45'S 170°12'E
Cook Is. Pacific Ocean **107 F3**
Cooper Creek r. Australia **106 B4**
Copenhagen Denmark **100 E4** 55°40'N 12°35'E
Coppermine North West Territories Canada **94 G2** 67°49'N 115°12'W
Connecticut st. USA **95 K4**
Coral Sea Pacific Ocean **106 C3**
Córdoba Argentina **97 F8** 31°25'S 64°10'W
Cork Ireland **100 C5** 51°54'N 8°28'W
Corrientes Argentina **97 G7** 27°30'S 58°48'W

Corsica i. France **100 D7** 40°00'N 9°10'E
Costa Rica Central America **96 D3**
Cotopaxi mt. Ecuador **96 E5** 0°40'S 78°28'W
Craiova Romania **101 F8** 44°18'N 23°46'E
Crete i. Greece **101 F7** 35°29'N 24°42'E
Croatia Europe **101 E6**
Cuba Central America **96 E2**
Curacao i. South America **96 F3** 12°15'N 69°00'W
Curitiba Brazil **97 H7** 25°24'S 49°16'W
Cuzco Peru **97 E6** 13°32'S 71°57'W
Cyprus Europe **101 G8**
Czechlands, The Europe **100-101 E6**

D
Dakar Senegal **98 A3** 14°38'N 17°27'W
Dalian China **105 J2** 38°53'N 121°37'E
Dallas Texas USA **95 I5** 32°47'N 96°48'W
Dalol Ethiopia **98 G3** 14°15'N 40°18'E
Damascus Syria **104 A2** 33°30'N 36°19'E
Da Nang Vietnam **105 H4** 16°04'N 108°13'E
Danube r. Europe **100-101 E6**
Dar es Salaam Tanzania **99 F5** 6°51'S 39°18'E
Darling r. Australia **106 C4**
Darwin Australia **106 B3** 12°23'S 130°44'E
Daugavpils Latvia **101 F4** 55°52'N 26°31'E
Davao Philippines **105 J5** 7°05'N 125°38'E
Davis Strait Greenland/Canada **95 M2**
De Aar South Africa **99 E8** 30°39'S 24°01'E
Deccan India **105 F4**
Delaware st. USA **95 K5**
Delhi India **104 E3** 28°40'N 77°13'E
Denmark Europe **100 D4**
Denver Colorado USA **94 H5** 39°43'N 105°01'W
Derby Australia **106 B3** 17°19'S 123°38'E
Detroit Michigan USA **95 J4** 42°20'N 83°03'W
Devon I. North West Territories Canada **95 J1** 75°00'N 86°00'W
Dhaka Bangladesh **105 G3** 23°43'N 90°25'E
Diré Dawa Ethiopia **98 G4** 9°35'N 41°50'E
Djibouti Africa **98 G3**
Djibouti Djibouti **98 G3** 11°35'N 43°11'E
Dnepr r. Ukraine **102 C4**
Dnepropetrovsk Ukraine **102 C4** 48°29'N 35°00'E
Dodoma Tanzania **99 F5** 6°10'S 35°40'E
Doha Qatar **104 C3** 25°15'N 51°34'E
Dominica Central America **96 F3**
Dominican Republic Central America **96 E3**
Don r. Russian Federation **102 D4**
Donetsk Ukraine **102 C4** 48°00'N 37°50'E
Dongola Sudan **98 F3** 19°10'N 30°27'E
Douala Cameroon **98 D4** 4°05'N 9°43'E
Douro r. Portugal **100 C7**
Drakensberg Mts. South Africa/Lesotho **99 E8**
Drava r. Yugoslavia **101 E6**
Dresden Germany **100 E5** 51°03'N 13°44'E
Dronning Maud Land Antarctica **109**
Dublin Ireland **100 C5** 53°21'N 6°18'W
Dunedin New Zealand **107 D5** 45°52'S 170°30'E
Durban South Africa **99 F7** 29°50'S 30°59'E
Dushanbe Tajikistan **102 F5** 38°38'N 68°51'E

E
East China Sea Asia **105 J2-J3**
East London South Africa **99 E8** 33°00'S 27°54'E
East Siberian Sea Arctic Ocean **103 O1-R1**
Ebro r. Spain **100 C7**
Ecuador South America **96 E4-E5**
Edinburgh UK **100 C4** 55°57'N 3°13'W
Edmonton Alberta Canada **94 G3** 53°30'N 113°30'W
Egypt Africa **98 E2**
El Aaiün Western Sahara **98 A2** 27°09'13°12'W
Elâzig Turkey **101 G8** 38°41'N 39°14'E
Elbe r. Germany **100 E5**
Elbert, Mt. Colorado USA **95 H5** 39°07'N 106°27'W
Elbrus mt. Europe (Russian Federation) **101 H7** 43°21'N 42°29'E
Ellesmere I. North West Territories Canada **95 J1** 78°00'N 82°00'W
Ellsworth Land Antarctica **109**
El Obeid Sudan **98 F3** 13°11'N 30°10'E
El Paso Texas USA **94 H5** 31°45'N 106°29'W
El Salvador Central America **96 D3**
Emi Koussi mt. Chad **98 D3** 19°58'N 18°30'E
Enderby Land Antarctica **109**

English Channel Europe **100 C5-D5**
Entebbe Uganda **99 F4** 0°08'N 32°29'E
Enugu Nigeria **98 C4** 6°20'N 7°29'E
Equatorial Guinea Africa **99 D4**
Esbjerg Denmark **100 D4** 55°28'N 8°27'E
Esperance Australia **106 B4** 33°49'S 121°52'E
Espiritu Santo i. Vanuatu **107 D3** 15°50'S 166°50'E
Es Samara Western Sahara **98 A2** 26°44'N 14°41'W
Estonia Europe **101 F4**
Ethiopia Africa **98 F4-G4**
Euphrates r. Asia **104 A2-B2**
Everest, Mt. China/Nepal **105 F3** 27°59'N 86°56'E
Eyre, Lake Australia **106 B4** 28°30'S 137°25'E

F
Faeroe Is. Denmark **100 C3**
Fairbanks Alaska USA **94 D2** 64°50'N 147°50'W
Falkland Is. Atlantic Ocean **97 G10**
Farewell, Cape Greenland **95 N2** 60°00'N 44°20'W
Fiji Pacific Ocean **107 E3**
Finland Europe **101 F3**
Finland, Gulf of Europe **101 F4**
Firat r. Turkey **101 G8**
Florence Italy **100 E7** 43°46'N 11°15'E
Flores i. Indonesia **105 J6** 8°40'S 121°20'E
Florida st. USA **95 J6**
Fortaleza Brazil **96 I5** 3°45'S 38°35'W
Fort Rupert Québec Canada **95 K3** 51°29'N 78°45'W
France Europe **100 D6**
Frankfurt Germany **100 D5** 50°07'N 8°40'E
Franz Josef Land is. Russian Federation **108**
Fraser r. British Columbia Canada **94 F3**
Freetown Sierra Leone **98 A4** 8°30'N 13°17'W
Freiburg Germany **100 D6** 47°59'N 7°51'E
Fremantle Australia **106 A4** 32°07'S 115°44'E
French Guiana South America **96 G4**
Frobisher Bay North West Territories Canada **95 L2** 63°45'N 68°30'W
Fukuoka Japan **105 J2** 33°39'N 130°21'E
Funafuti Tuvalu **107 D3** 8°31'S 179°13'E
Fushun China **105 J1** 41°50'N 123°55'E
Fuzhou China **105 I3** 26°09'N 119°21'E

G
Gabès Tunisia **98 D1** 33°53'N 10°07'E
Gabon Africa **99 D5**
Galapagos Is. Ecuador **96 C5**
Gambia, The Africa **98 A3**
Gambier Is. Pacific Ocean **107 G4** 23°10'S 135°00'W
Ganges r. India **105 F3**
Garoua Cameroon **98 D4** 9°17'N 13°22'E
Gdansk Poland **101 E5** 54°22'N 18°38'E
Geneva Switzerland **100 D6** 46°12'N 6°09'E
Genoa Italy **100 D7** 44°25'N 8°57'E
Georgetown Guyana **96 G4** 6°46'N 58°10'W
George Town Malaysia **105 H5** 5°30'N 100°16'E
Georgia Europe **101 H7**
Georgia st. USA **95 J5**
Ghadamis Libya **98 C1** 30°08'N 9°30'E
Ghana Africa **98 B4**
Ghardaïa Algeria **98 C1** 32°29'N 3°40'E
Ghat Libya **98 D2** 24°58'N 10°11'E
Gibraltar Europe **100 C8** 36°09'N 5°21'W
Gijón Spain **100 C7** 43°32'N 5°40'W
Gilbert Is. Kiribati **107 D3**
Glâma r. Norway **100 E3**
Glasgow UK **100 C4** 55°52'N 4°15'W
Gobi Desert Asia **105 G1-H1**
Godávari r. India **104 E4**
Godhavn Greenland **95 M2** 69°20'N 53°30'W
Godthåb see Nuuk
Goiânia Brazil **97 H6** 16°43'S 49°18'W
Gomel Belorussia **102 C3** 52°25'N 31°00'E
Good Hope, Cape of Africa **99 D8** 34°21'S 18°28'E
Goose Bay Newfoundland Canada **95 L3** 53°19'N 60°24'W
Gora Pobeda mt. Russian Federation **103 N2** 65°10'N 146°00'E
Gothenburg Sweden **100 E4** 57°43'N 11°58'E
Gotland i. Sweden **101 E4** 57°30'N 18°33'E
Gran Chaco South America **97 F7**
Grand Bahama i. Bahamas **96 E2** 26°40'N 78°20'W
Grand Cayman i. Central America **96 D3** 19°20'N 81°30'W
Graz Austria **100 E6** 47°05'N 15°27'E
Great Australian Bight Australia **106 B4**

Luzon i. Philippines **105 J4** 17°50'N 121°00'E
Lvov Ukraine **102 B4** 49°50'N 24°00'E

M
Macapa Brazil **96 G5** 0°04'N 51°04'W
Macau Asia **105 I3** 22°11'N 113°33'E
MacKenzie r. Canada **94 F2**
Madagascar Africa **99 G7**
Madang Papua New Guinea **106 C3** 5°14'S 145°45'E
Madeira i. Africa **98 A1** 32°45'N 17°00'W
Madeira r. Brazil **96 F5**
Madras India **104 E4** 13°05'N 80°18'E
Madrid Spain **100 C7** 40°24'N 3°41'W
Magadan Russian Federation **103 O3** 59°38'N 150°50'E
Magellan's Strait Chile **97 F10**
Mahajanga Madagascar **99 G6** 15°43'S 46°19'E
Maiduguri Nigeria **98 D3** 11°53'N 13°16'E
Maine st. USA **95 L4**
Majorca i. Spain **100 D8** 39°30'N 3°00'E
Malabo Equatorial Guinea **98 C4** 3°45'N 8°48'E
Malaga Spain **100 C8** 36°43'N 4°25'W
Malakal Sudan **99 F4** 9°31'N 31°39'E
Malanje Angola **99 D5** 9°36'S 16°21'E
Malawi Africa **99 F6**
Malaysia Asia **105 H5**
Maldives Indian Ocean **104 E5**
Male Maldives **104 E5** 4°00'N 73°28'E
Mali Africa **98 B3**
Malmö Sweden **100 E4** 55°36'N 13°00'E
Malta Europe **100 E8**
Maluku is. Indonesia **105 J5** 4°00'S 129°00'E
Man, Isle of UK **100 C5** 54°15'N 4°30'W
Managua Nicaragua **96 D3** 12°06'N 81°18'W
Manaus Brazil **96 F5** 3°06'S 60°00'W
Manchester UK **100 C5** 53°30'N 2°15'W
Manila Philippines **105 J4** 14°36'N 120°59'E
Manitoba st. Canada **95 I3**
Maputo Mozambique **99 F7** 25°58'S 32°35'E
Marabá Brazil **96 H5** 5°23'S 49°10'W
Maracaibo Venezuela **96 E3** 10°44'N 71°37'W
Maramba Zambia **99 E6** 17°40'S 25°50'E
Mar del Plata Argentina **97 G8** 38°00'S 57°32'W
Marie Byrd Land Antarctica **109**
Marka Somalia **99 G4** 1°42'N 44°47'E
Marquesas Is. Pacific Ocean **107 G3**
Marrakech Morocco **98 B1** 31°49'N 8°00'W
Marshall Is. Pacific Ocean **107 D2**
Marseille France **100 D7** 43°18'N 5°24'E
Martinique i. Central America **96 F3** 14°40'N 61°00'W
Maryland st. USA **95 K5**
Maseru Lesotho **99 E7** 29°18'S 27°28'E
Mashhad Iran **104 C2** 36°16'N 59°34'E
Massachusetts st. USA **95 K4**
Massif Central mts. France **100 D7**
Matamoros Mexico **96 C2** 25°32'N 103°15'W
Mato Grosso Brazil **97 G6**
Matterhorn mt. Switzerland/Italy **D6 100** 45°59'N 7°43'E
Mauritania Africa **98 A3**
Mauritius Indian Ocean **93 P8**
Mayotte i. Comoros **99 G6** 12°50'S 45°10'E
Mazatlán Mexico **96 B2** 23°13'N 106°25'W
Mbabane Swaziland **99 F7** 26°19'S 31°08'E
Mbala Zambia **99 F5** 8°53'S 31°24'E
Mbuji-Mayi Zaire **99 E5** 6°08'S 23°39'E
McKinley, Mt. Alaska USA **94 C2** 63°00'N 151°00'W
Mecca Saudi Arabia **104 B3** 21°26'N 39°49'E
Medan Indonesia **105 G5** 3°35'N 98°39'E
Medellín Colombia **96 E4** 6°15'N 75°36'W
Mediterranean Sea Europe/Africa **100 D8**
Meknès Morocco **98 B1** 33°53'N 5°37'W
Mekong r. Asia **105 H4**
Melanesia is. Pacific Ocean **106 D3**
Melbourne Australia **106 C4** 37°45'S 144°58'E
Melilla Spain **100 C8** 35°17'N 2°57'W
Melville I. Canada **94 G1** 75°30'N 110°00'W
Memphis Tennessee USA **95 J5** 35°08'N 90°03'W
Mendoza Argentina **97 F8** 32°54'S 68°50'W
Menongue Angola **99 D6** 14°40'S 17°41'E
Mérida Mexico **96 D2** 20°59'N 89°39'W
Mersin Turkey **101 G8** 36°47'N 34°37'E
Mexicali Mexico **96 A1** 32°40'N 115°29'W
Mexico Central America **96 B2**
Mexico, Gulf of North America **95 I6-J6**
Mexico City Mexico **96 C3** 19°25'N 99°10'W
Mezen Russian Federation **102 D2** 65°50'N 44°20'E

Miami Florida USA **95 J6** 25°45'N 80°15'W
Michigan st. USA **95 J4**
Michigan, Lake USA **95 J4** 44°00'N 87°00'W
Micronesia is. Pacific Ocean **106 C2**
Midway Is. Hawaiian Is. **107 E1**
Milan Italy **100 D6** 45°28'N 9°12'E
Milwaukee Wisconsin USA **95 J4** 43°02'N 87°55'W
Mindanao i. Philippines **105 J5** 7°30'N 125°00'E
Minneapolis Minnesota USA **95 I4** 44°59'N 93°13'W
Minnesota st. USA **95 I4**
Minsk Belorussia **102 B3** 53°51'N 27°30'E
Mississippi r. USA **95 I4-I5**
Mississippi st. USA **95 J5**
Missouri r. Nebraska USA **95 I4**
Missouri st. USA **95 I5**
Moçambique Mozambique **99 G6** 15°00'S 40°47'E
Mogadishu Somalia **99 G4** 2°02'N 45°21'E
Moldavia Europe **102 B4**
Monaco Europe **100 D7**
Monclova Mexico **96 B2** 26°54'N 101°25'W
Mongolia Asia **105 G1-H1**
Monrovia Liberia **98 A4** 6°20'N 10°46'W
Montana st. USA **94 H4**
Monterrey Mexico **96 B2** 25°40'N 100°19'W
Montevideo Uruguay **97 G8** 34°53'S 56°11'W
Montréal Québec Canada **95 K4** 45°31'N 73°34'W
Mopti Mali **98 B3** 14°29'N 4°10'W
Morocco Africa **98 B1**
Moroni Comoros **99 G6** 11°40'S 43°19'E
Moscow Russian Federation **102 C3** 55°45'N 37°42'E
Mosul Iraq **104 B2** 36°21'N 43°08'E
Mount Gambier Australia **106 C4** 37°51'S 140°50'E
Mozambique Africa **99 F6**
Mozambique Channel Indian Ocean **99 G6**
Mtwara Tanzania **99 G6** 10°17'S 40°11'E
Munich Germany **100 E6** 48°08'N 11°34'E
Murmansk Russian Federation **102 C2** 68°59'N 33°08'E
Murray r. Australia **106 C4**
Murzuq Libya **98 D2** 22°55'N 13°55'E
Muscat Oman **104 C3** 23°36'N 58°37'E
Mwanza Kenya **99 F5** 7°51'S 26°43'E
Mwaya Tanzania **99 F5** 9°33'S 33°56'E
Myanmar (Burma) Asia **105 G3**

N
Nagpur India **104 E3** 21°09'N 79°06'E
Nairobi Kenya **99 F5** 1°17'S 36°50'E
Namibe Angola **99 D6** 15°10'S 12°09'E
Namibia Africa **99 D7**
Nampula Mozambique **99 F6** 15°09'S 39°14'E
Nanchang China **105 I3** 28°37'N 115°57'E
Nan Shan mts. China **105 G2**
Nantes France **100 C6** 47°13'N 1°33'W
Naples Italy **100 E7** 40°51'N 14°17'E
Narvik Norway **101 E2** 68°26'N 17°25'E
Nassau Bahamas **96 E2** 25°05'N 77°21'W
Nasser, Lake Egypt **98 F2** 22°40'N 32°00'E
Natal Brazil **96 I5** 5°46'S 35°15'W
Nauru Pacific Ocean **107 D3**
Ndélé Central African Republic **98 E4** 8°24'N 20°39'E
N'Djamena Chad **98 D3** 12°10'N 14°59'E
Ndola Zambia **99 E6** 12°58'S 28°39'E
Nebraska st. USA **95 I4**
Negro r. Brazil **96 F5**
Nelson r. Manitoba Canada **95 I3**
Nepal Asia **105 F3**
Netherlands Europe **100 D5**
Nevada st. USA **94 G5**
New Brunswick st. Canada **95 L4**
New Caledonia is. Pacific Ocean **107 D3**
Newcastle Australia **106 C4** 32°55'S 151°46'E
New Delhi India **105 E3** 28°36'N 77°12'E
New Georgia Is. Solomon Is. **107 C3**
New Guinea i. Australasia **106 B3** 5°00'S 140°00'E
Newfoundland st. Canada **95 M3**
New Hampshire st. USA **95 K4**
New Jersey st. USA **95 K4**
New Mexico st. USA **95 H5**
New Orleans Louisiana USA **95 I6** 29°58'N 90°07'W
New Siberian Is. Russian Federation **103 M1-N1**
New South Wales st. Australia **106 C4**
New York st. USA **95 K4**
New York New York USA **95 K4** 40°43'N 74°01'W
New Zealand Australasia **107 D5**
Niamey Niger **98 C3** 13°32'N 2°05'E
Nicaragua Central America **96 D3**

Nice France **100 D7** 43°42'N 7°16'E
Nicosia Cyprus **101 G8** 35°11'N 33°23'E
Niger Africa **98 C3-D3**
Niger r. Africa **98 C4**
Nigeria Africa **98 C4**
Nile Egypt **98 F2**
Niue i. Cook Is. **107 E3** 19°02'S 169°52'W
Nizhneangarsk Russian Federation **103 K3** 55°48'N 109°35'E
Nizhnevartovsk Russian Federation **102 G2** 60°57'N 76°40'E
Nizhniy Novgorod Russian Federation **102 D3** 56°20'N 44°00'E
Nordvik Russian Federation **103 K1** 73°40'N 110°50'E
Norfolk Virginia USA **95 K5** 36°54'N 76°18'W
Norfolk I. Pacific Ocean **107 D4** 29°02'S 167°57'E
Noril'sk Russian Federation **102 H2** 69°21'N 88°02'E
Normanton Australia **106 C3** 17°40'S 141°05'E
North Cape New Zealand **107 D4** 34°23'S 173°04'E
North Carolina st. USA **95 K5**
North Dakota st. USA **95 I4**
North Dvina r. Russian Federation **102 D2**
Northern Marianas is. Pacific Ocean **106 C1-C2**
Northern Territory st. Australia **106 B3**
North I. New Zealand **107 D4** 38°00'S 175°00'E
North Magnetic Pole (1985) Arctic Ocean **108**
North Pole Arctic Ocean **108** 90°00'N
North Sea Europe **100 D4**
North West Territories st. Canada **94-95 G2-I2**
Norway Europe **100 D3**
Norwegian Dependency Antarctica **109**
Norwegian Sea Europe **100 D3**
Nouadhibou Mauritania **98 A2** 20°54'N 17°01'W
Nouakchott Mauritania **98 A3** 18°09'N 15°58'W
Nova Iguaçu Brazil **97 H7** 22°45'S 43°27'W
Nova Scotia st. Canada **95 L4**
Novaya Zemlya i. Russian Federation **102 E1** 74°00'N 56°00'E
Novgorod Russian Federation **102 C3** 58°30'N 31°20'E
Novosibirsk Russian Federation **102 H3** 55°05'N 83°05'E
Nuevo Laredo Mexico **96 C2** 27°30'N 99°31'W
Nukualofa Tonga **107 E3** 21°07'S 175°12'W
Nuuk Greenland **95 M2** 64°10'N 51°40'W
Nyasa, Lake Malawi **99 F6** 12°00'S 34°30'E

O
Ob r. Russian Federation **102 H3**
Ob, Gulf of Russian Federation **102 G2**
Oder r. Poland **101 E5**
Odessa Ukraine **102 C4** 46°30'N 30°46'E
Ohio r. USA **95 J5**
Ohio st. USA **95 J5**
Okhotsk, Sea of Russian Federation **102 N3-O3**
Oklahoma st. USA **95 I5**
Oklahoma City Oklahoma USA **95 I5** 35°28'N 97°32'W
Olekminsk Russian Federation **103 L2** 60°25'N 120°00'E
Olenëk Russian Federation **103 L2** 68°38'N 112°15'E
Omaha Nebraska USA **95 I4** 41°16'N 95°57'W
Oman Asia **104 C3**
Omdurman Sudan **98 F3** 15°37'N 32°59'E
Omsk Russian Federation **102 G3** 55°00'N 73°22'E
Onega, Lake Russian Federation **102 C2** 62°00'N 35°30'E
Ontario st. Canada **95 J3**
Oporto Portugal **100 C7** 41°11'N 8°36'W
Oran Algeria **98 B1** 35°42'N 0°38'W
Orange r. South Africa **99 D7**
Oregon st. USA **94 F4**
Orenburg Russian Federation **102 E3** 51°50'N 55°00'E
Orinoco r. Venezuela **96 F4**
Orkney Is. UK **100 C4**
Osaka Japan **105 K2** 34°40'N 135°30'E
Oslo Norway **100 E4** 59°55'N 10°45'E
Ottawa Ontario Canada **95 K4** 45°25'N 75°42'W
Ouagadougou Burkina Faso **98 B3** 12°20'N 1°40'W
Oudtshoorn South Africa **99 E8** 33°35'S 22°11'E
Oujda Morocco **98 B1** 34°41'N 1°45'W
Oulu Finland **101 F2** 65°01'N 25°28'E

P
Pacific Ocean **92 B7**
Padang Indonesia **105 H6** 0°55'S 100°21'E
Pago Pago i. Pacific Ocean **107 E3** 14°16'S 170°42'W
Pakistan Asia **104 D3**
Palau Is. Pacific Ocean **106 B2**

Index

Where a page number is in **bold type**, this means it is a main entry for this word.

Universal Edition
First published in 1992 by Usborne
Publishing Ltd, Usborne House, 83-85
Saffron Hill, London EC1N 8RT, England.
Copyright © 1992 Usborne Publishing Ltd.

First published in America March 1993
The name Usborne and the device 🗫 are
Trade Marks of Usborne Publishing Ltd. All
rights reserved. No part of this publication
may be reproduced, stored in a retrieval